THE
RACECAR
Book

THE RACECAR *Book*

BUILD AND RACE MOUSETRAP CARS, DRAGSTERS, TRI-CAN HAULERS *& More*

BOBBY MERCER

CHICAGO REVIEW PRESS

Copyright © 2013 by Bobby Mercer
First edition
Published by Chicago Review Press, Incorporated
814 North Franklin Street
Chicago, Illinois 60610
ISBN 978-1-61374-714-8

Library of Congress Cataloging-in-Publication Data
Mercer, Bobby, 1961- author.
   The racecar book : build and race mousetrap cars, dragsters, tri-can haulers,
and more / Bobby Mercer. — First edition.
      pages cm
   Audience: 9+
   ISBN 978-1-61374-714-8 (pbk.)
   1. Model car racing—Juvenile literature. 2. Automobiles,
Racing—Models—Juvenile literature. I. Title.

   GV1570.M47 2013
   629.22'18—dc23

                                                    2013024944

Cover design: Andrew Brozyna, AJB Design, Inc.
Interior design: Rattray Design
Photo credits: Bobby Mercer

Printed in the United States of America
5 4 3 2 1

Contents

7 *Racecar Launchers* 181

Introduction

Ever since the first cavemen decided to leave their caves, humans have searched for new ways to move. The wheel allowed mankind to move faster across the landscape, and wheels led to racing.

Racing cars is a sport that never grows old. Mousetrap-powered cars, rubber band–powered racers, and edible car contests are common in science and technology classes. Contest hints and ideas are given for each type of car found in this book. Many cars on these pages are easily adaptable for science fair projects. Have fun, experiment, and change any of these designs—you're the engineer!

Most of all, homemade cars are a blast to play with. Just think of yourself as an early racing pioneer as you build and race these vehicles. Many of the racecars can be built with stuff easily found in the house or garage. Some involve a trip to the hardware store, but all are easy to build.

For Teachers

The curiosity created by building and testing cars may lead a child into the arena of science, technology, engineering, and math—commonly called STEM. And classes designed to emphasize STEM ideals are at the forefront of our educational system.

1

The Starting Line

Do you feel the need . . . the need for speed? Racing cars is just fun, and building your own racecars adds to the excitement. But science is also involved in building and racing cars. If you want to build away, go ahead—you can always come back to this chapter later. But knowing about the science involved in your racecars is the key to making cars that roll farther and faster.

Ways to Power Your Racecar

Cars need energy to go. In a traditional car, that energy comes from gasoline. In the future more and more cars will run on electricity from batteries. But for the cars you are going to build, you will be using free and renewable sources of energy—rubber bands, mousetraps, chemical reactions, air pressure, and gravity. The key is getting that energy to spin the wheels.

How to Make Great Racecars

Friction is important for a good racecar. Friction is a force that opposes motion, but friction also keeps the wheels from spinning in place. A racecar driver never wants a wheel that spins in place.

Friction depends on two things: weight and the types of surfaces in contact. Rubber is a great material because it provides a lot of friction, which is why you play basketball, volleyball, and tennis in rubber-soled shoes. Wrapping a rubber band or a piece of a balloon around your wheels can increase friction, and off your car will go.

Weight is a tricky thing with your car. Too much weight and it won't go very far. But too little weight and the wheels will just spin in place. Adding weights like coins and soda cans may actually make some cars roll farther. Experiment to find the best combination to help your car go.

The key to science is experimentation. Feel free to modify any of the plans in this book if you have a better idea; you won't know unless you try.

Wheels

To roll, you need wheels. Save every round thing you come across: CDs, bottle caps, jar lids, and plastic can covers (like those from Pringles cans) all work well. Another great source for wheels is old toys. Save the wheels from any broken toy before you recycle the rest. A relatively cheap and lightweight wheel can be found in stores that sell fake flowers. Round Styrofoam discs are used in floral arrangements and also make great lightweight wheels. You can also buy wheels at hobby stores, which sell a large variety of wheels for remote control cars and planes.

For maximum speed and distance, store-bought wheels are hard to beat. Many are made from high density foam, which leads to lightweight tires and great friction that blast off from the starting line. But store-bought wheels take cash and planning. Every racecar in this book can also be built with free wheels. Keep a box in your room with anything you might be able to use. If it's round, save it. Someday you may use it to help create world record racecars.

Growing up, my brother and I had to hide stuff from our trash monster: my sweet mom. She would have been more understanding if we had just explained the benefit of creative construction.

Axles

All wheels need axles. Axles can be fixed or rotating. A fixed axle is stationary; the wheel spins on the axle. A rotating axle is affixed to the wheel, and the entire wheel and axle combination spins.

Regardless of type, toothpicks and bamboo skewers make great axles. Bamboo skewers are toothpicks on steroids. Your parents may already have these around the house. They are also available at dollar, grocery, and big box stores. You can also buy metal rods or wooden dowels at most home improvement stores. They add to the cost, but sometimes it is worth it for a contest.

Contests

Mousetrap car contests are a great way for science to come alive. Designing and building a mousetrap car is fun and educational. Mousetrap car contests have one of two goals: the fastest speed or the longest distance. Modify your mousetrap car to achieve maximum results for your specific contest.

Another type of car contest is an edible racing battle, in which the car must be made primarily from edible parts. Fun, educational, and tasty! The rules may allow for toothpicks or skewers, so read the rules carefully. Regardless of contest type, you need to learn a little about energy so you can achieve the best results.

Energy

Energy is the ability to do work. And in science, work means getting something to move. Energy comes in two forms: potential and kinetic. Potential energy (PE) is stored energy. A stretched rubber band has stored elastic potential energy. Elastic materials will return to their original shape after being stretched. Elastic energy is most commonly found in rubber bands and springs. You will use both to power your racecars.

A box sitting on a high shelf has stored gravitational potential energy. Gravitational potential energy is energy an object has because of its position. Climbing a flight of stairs gives you more potential energy. Ramps will be used to give a few of your racecars the energy they need to go.

Once your car starts moving, the potential energy is converted into kinetic energy (KE, or energy of motion). The more stored energy you have, the greater kinetic energy you will get out. Play with a rubber band to understand this. Stretch it a little and shoot it. Now stretch it more and shoot it. More PE equals more KE, and KE means speed. And speed is fun.

2
Mousetrap Cars

Mousetrap cars—rolling machines powered by the spring of a mousetrap—are a ton of fun. Car design is crucial as you shoot for a world record distance or a world record speed. If you want a little more power, you can even go with a rattrap.

Mousetrap car contests are popular events for science olympiads. Participants are asked to build a car that will roll the greatest distance powered only by a single mousetrap. Adding a longer lever arm to the spring is the best way to create maximum distance. Other contests just measure speed over a set distance. If you participate in a mousetrap car competition, be sure to read the rules carefully. You will probably need to make a trip to the hardware or hobby store in order to create the best racecar possible, but there are a few plans that use mostly free and recycled stuff you already have around the house.

Take a close look at a mousetrap. A mousetrap consists of a wooden base, a spring, a hammer, a catch, and a holding bar. The energy of a mousetrap car comes from the spring. The metal spring is coiled around the base of a square called the hammer. The hammer is the part that snaps closed when the mousetrap is sprung by a cheese-loving rodent.

A basic mousetrap also contains a catch, which is the platform for the cheese, and a holding bar, which holds the loaded mousetrap hammer until a mouse samples the cheese. You will only use the spring and the hammer for your cars. The holding bar and catch will be removed to save weight.

Wheel choice is very important on a mousetrap car, since bigger wheels will cover a greater distance each time they rotate. Think of the bicycles you have owned. As you grew, the wheels grew too and you covered more distance. Old CDs are probably your best free choice for wheels—the perfect way to repurpose discs that are no longer needed. Also, when you buy a package of blank CDs, they often come with at least one clear CD-sized plastic top (or bottom) to protect the actual CDs. These layers make great wheels, as they are even lighter than the CDs. Of course, many hobby stores sell lightweight remote control car wheels. These wheels are designed for speed and traction, but they will cost you.

Rubber faucet washers work the best to hold the CDs onto the axles. They are beveled and large enough to fill the CD center hole. They can be found in the plumbing section of any hardware store or large department store. Wooden dowels should be available in the same stores. A dowel with a 3/16-inch diameter works the best, but other sizes will also work. Take the dowel to the plumbing department and you can find a washer that will fit snugly around it.

Balloons or glue can be used to increase the traction on the wheels. This is another great way to increase distance. Adding lubricants to the axles will help the car roll easier; WD-40 and graphite powder are great choices for this. You will also need some scrap wood to attach to the car for size. For a mousetrap contest, lightweight wood is important. Balsa wood—the wood used in model airplanes—is the best choice because it has enormous strength for its weight. Balsa wood is available at all craft and hobby stores.

Many hobby stores and websites also sell mousetrap car kits. These kits will give you all the basic pieces and eliminate the need for much adult help. Kits are fun, but they can limit your creativity. A list of kit makers and websites is included at the end of this chapter.

Mousetrap cars can also be a great choice for science fair projects. Science fairs expect you to design an experiment and take measurements to reach a conclusion. Mousetrap cars are fun to build, and the distance they roll is easy to measure. You can vary the length of the lever arm or the wheel diameter and measure the rolling distance for each variation. You can also compare a rattrap car to a mousetrap car. Rattraps are larger and weigh more, but they have a more powerful spring. However, rattrap cars won't be allowed in most contests. Nevertheless, they are fun to build and play with.

Now it's time to start building some cars.

CHEESE WAGON

This basic design will get you started launching mousetrap cars.

Adult supervision required

Rolling Gear

Standard mousetrap

Needle-nose pliers

Small piece of wood

Drill

Handsaw

Wood glue

4 screw eyes

Wooden dowel

Faucet washers

Superglue

4 old CDs

Fishing line or thread

Tape or cable ties

Step 1: Use needle-nose pliers to remove the mousetrap's holding bar. The holding bar is the long, straight bar that allows you to set the mousetrap.

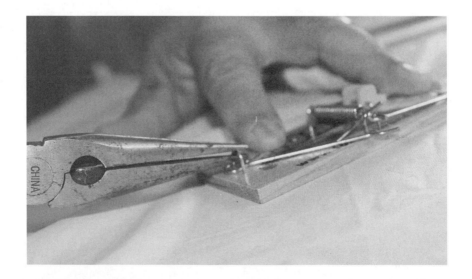

Step 2: Use the pliers to remove the catch. The catch is the platform for the cheese bait.

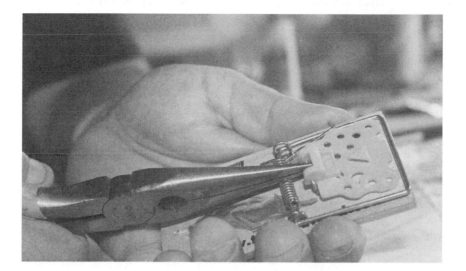

Step 3: With an adult's help, drill a ½-inch hole in the end of a piece of wood near one end. This piece of wood will be glued to the base of the mousetrap. The piece shown is 2½ inches by 6 inches, but the size of the piece can vary, so just use what you have. Any type of wood will work, but for a contest balsa is the best choice, since it is very light. But using balsa may mean a trip to the hobby store.

Step 4: With an adult's help, use a handsaw to cut from the end to each side of the hole. You will be left with a ½-inch-wide, U-shaped cutout from one end.

Step 5: Use wood glue to secure the mousetrap to the wooden base you just created. Make sure the U extends past the end of the mousetrap. Let the glue dry for a few hours.

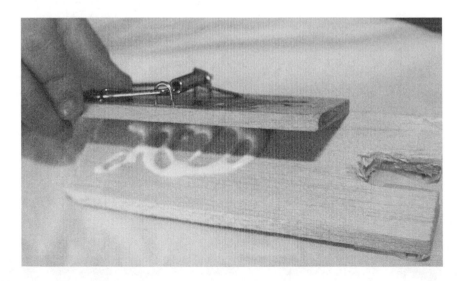

Step 6: Once the glue is dry, put a screw eye into the bottom of each corner of the wooden base.

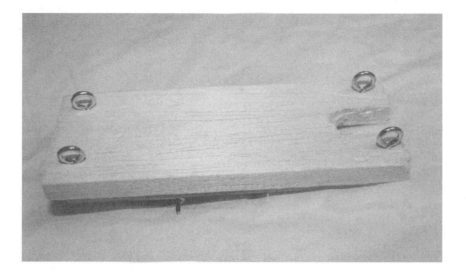

Step 7: Cut your dowel a few inches longer than the width of your base wood block. Slide a faucet washer onto the dowel with the beveled side pointing out. Cut another axle out of the dowel for the front wheels. Set one piece aside.

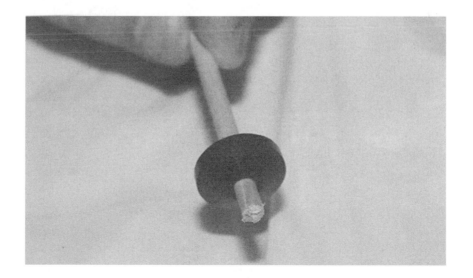

Step 8: Have an adult put superglue on the beveled side of the washer.

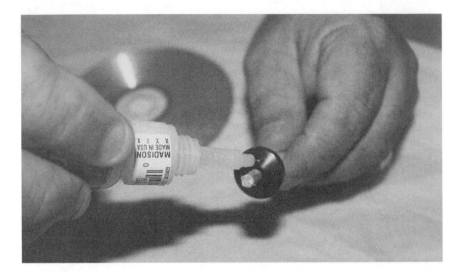

Step 9: Before the glue dries, quickly slide a CD onto the dowel so that it is on the beveled side of the washer and center the washer in the hole.

Step 10: Slide another faucet washer onto the dowel with the flat side toward the CD. Press it onto the CD and make sure it is centered. Let the superglue dry for at least 5 minutes.

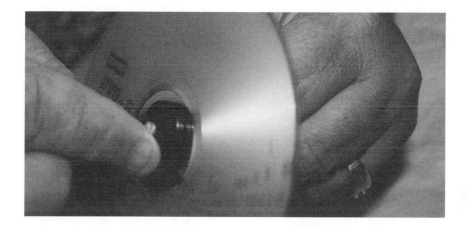

Step 11: Slide another washer on the axle with the beveled side toward the mousetrap and the flat side toward the CD wheel. Slide the wheel axle combination through the rear set of screw eyes. The rear of the car is the end with the U. Slide another faucet washer onto the other end of the axle with the bevel toward the mousetrap to secure the axle in place.

Step 12: It is easier to do this step before you put the other rear wheel on. Tie a 20-inch-long piece of fishing line or thread to the rear axle in the cut-out U. Use a cable tie, zip tie, or tape to secure your knot. The fishing line can just dangle while you finish the rest of the construction.

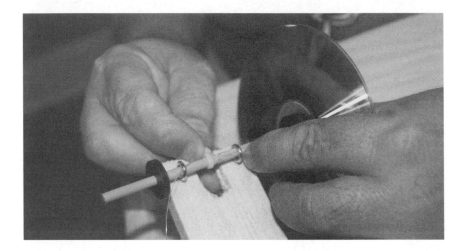

Step 13: Slide another washer onto the axle with the beveled side out. With adult help, superglue another rear wheel on the other end of the rear axle. Secure with another washer, with its flat side toward the wheel.

Step 14: Make sure the wheels are parallel to each other and straight up and down. Let the glue dry for at least 5 minutes before starting on the front axle.

Step 15: Repeat Steps 9 through 11 on the front axle. You may need to shorten the axle depending on the length of your wooden base. Set aside for at least 10 minutes to let all the glue dry before getting ready to launch your Cheese Wagon.

Step 16: Tie the free end of the fishing line or thread to the middle of the spring hammer on the mousetrap. You will probably want to secure the knot with tape or a cable tie.

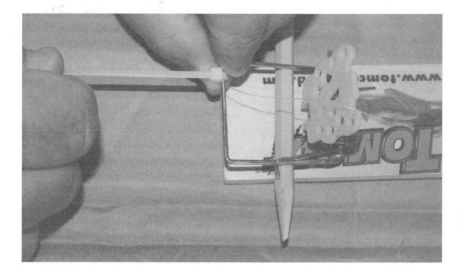

Step 17: Pull the spring hammer toward the rear and slowly wind the fishing line or thread around the rear axle.

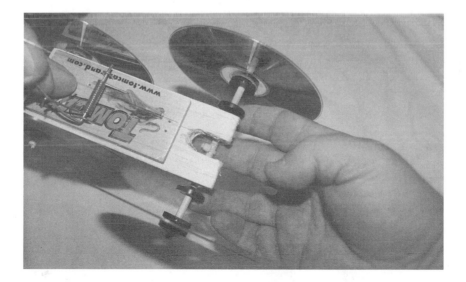

Step 18: Place the car on the floor and let the spring hammer go.

Additional Racecar Topics

You can increase friction on any wheels by adding rubber. You can do this easily with balloons. Blow up a balloon and let it deflate several times to stretch it out. Cut 4 slices across the balloon to create 4 large, circular straps. Stretch each piece of balloon around the edge of each CD.

TOP FUEL

Top Fuel is a long, sleek, rolling machine designed to travel over 50 feet.

Adult supervision required

Rolling Gear

Mousetrap

Needle-nose pliers

Brass tube, 12 inches long

Long piece of wood, 1 inch wide (balsa is best)

Pencil

Handsaw

Drill and bits

Wood glue

2 brass tubes or dowels with $3/16$ diameters, 6 inches long

Faucet washers

4 old CDs

Superglue

Duct tape (optional)

Fishing line or thread

Step 1: Use needle-nose pliers to remove the staple securing the mousetrap's holding bar, if present.

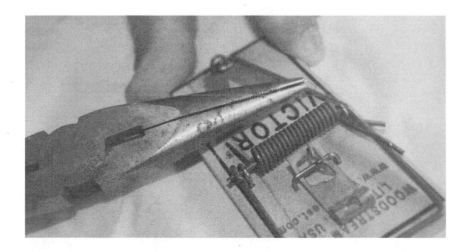

Step 2: Remove the holding bar to reduce weight, if allowed under competition rules. Some contests may require the car to be launched using the catch and holding bar. If both are required by rules, skip to Step 4.

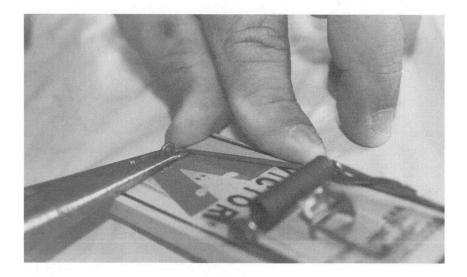

Step 3: Remove the catch as well.

Step 4: Use the needle-nose pliers to cut the spring hammer on one side of the square. Remove the short piece left and straighten out the long remaining piece.

Step 5: Lay your mousetrap and the long piece of brass tubing on the 1-inch-wide piece of balsa wood. Mark the length with a pencil and then cut 2 pieces to that length.

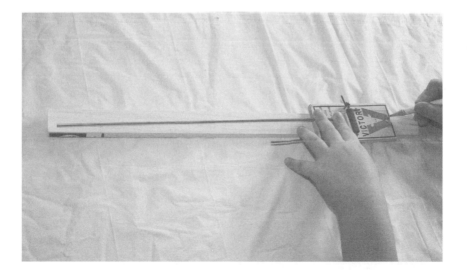

Step 6: Have an adult drill a ¼-inch hole in both boards, 1 inch from the end. Drill slowly in balsa wood because it is very light. These holes will hold the axles, so **they need to be drilled at the same time**, which will allow the axles to be perfectly parallel and perpendicular to the long side rails.

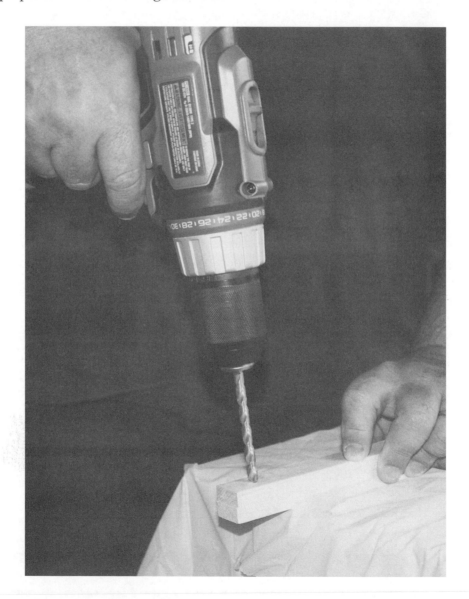

Step 7: At the end of each wooden rail, put 3 inches of wood glue along the narrow edge. This is the top of the rail.

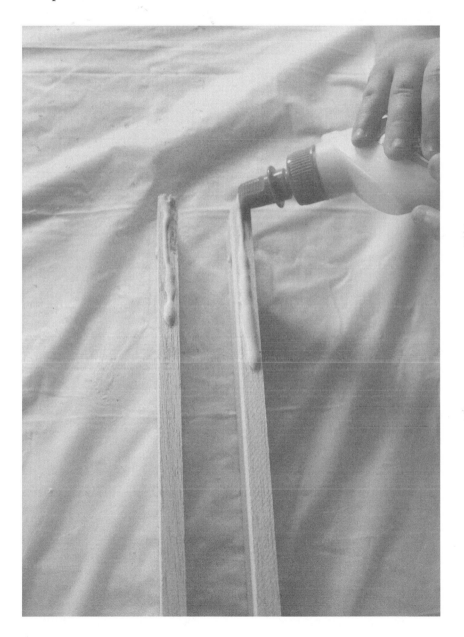

Step 8: Place the mousetrap on the glue with the loose spring hammer pointing toward the long end of the rails. Make sure that the rails are at the edge of the mousetrap and that the rails are perfectly parallel. Let this glue dry for at least 24 hours before you put the axles through to complete the Top Fuel. You can work on the wheels and axles while the glue dries.

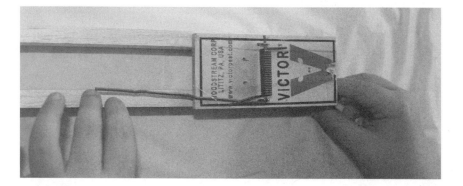

Step 9: Push one short brass tube through the center of a faucet washer. Repeat for the other brass tube. If you don't have a brass tube, ³⁄₁₆-inch dowels will also work.

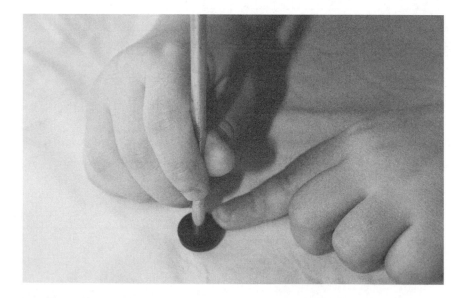

Step 10: Slide a faucet washer into the center hole of the CD. Many washers will fit very snugly and will not need superglue. If it fits snugly, you are done. If not, you will need to use a second washer to sandwich the CD, and possibly some superglue to hold the washers together.

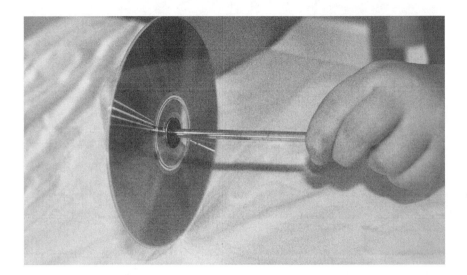

Step 11: Slide the long brass tube onto the straight piece of the spring hammer on the mousetrap. Friction should hold it in place. If you don't have a tube, you can use a 12-inch-long piece of dowel—use duct tape to secure it to the spring hammer.

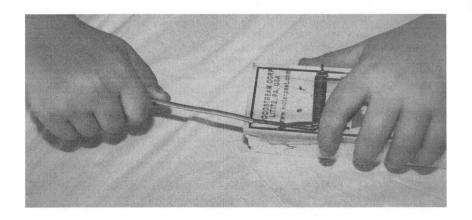

Step 12: Use needle-nose pliers to create a hook in the other end of the tube. If you used a dowel you can skip this step.

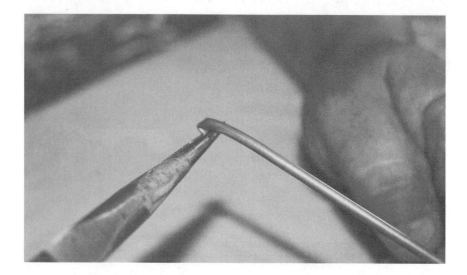

Step 13: Tie a long piece of fishing line or thread to the hook. If using a dowel, just tie it tightly to one end and secure with a small strip of duct tape.

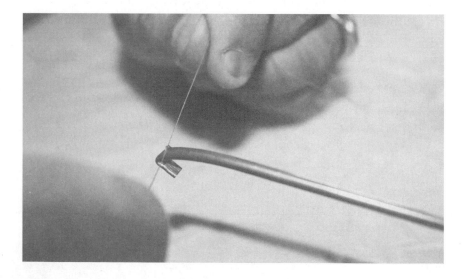

Step 14: Use the needle-nose pliers to bend the hook over to further capture the fishing line or thread end.

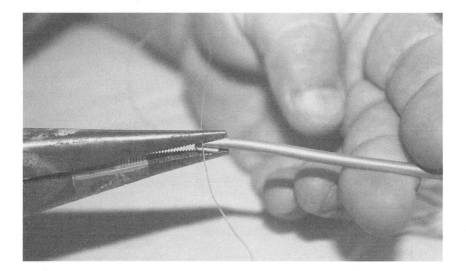

Step 15: After the glue on the rails has completely dried, slide one wheel-axle combination through the holes in both rails. Slide a faucet washer onto the other end and add glue (if needed).

Step 16: Slide a CD over the faucet washer. Repeat for the other wheel-axle combination.

Step 17: Cut the fishing line or thread about 6 inches longer than the dragster. The total length of the fishing line will be at least twice the length of the racecar.

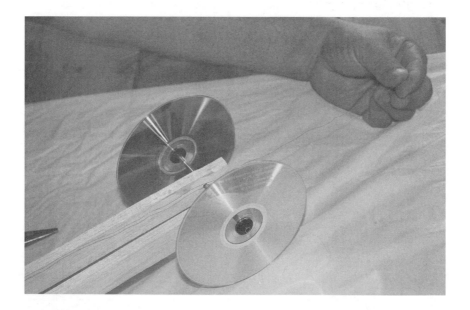

Step 18: Tie the other end tightly around the rear axle, between the rails.

Step 19: Secure the knot with a small piece of tape.

Step 20: Use your thumb and fingers to wind the loose fishing line or thread around the rear axle. Winding with the axle is better than applying force to the CD wheels.

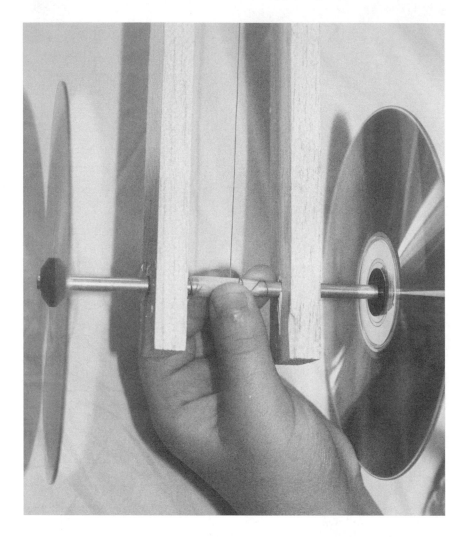

Step 21: With one hand, pull the spring hammer toward the rear wheel. Use the other hand to wind up the fishing line or thread. Continue winding until the spring hammer is tight down to the rails. You will need to hold the rails and spring hammer together to keep the wheels from spinning.

Step 22: Place the Top Fuel dragster on the floor, and leave plenty of room for the brass tube to swing forward. The front end is the end with the mousetrap. Let go of the tube and watch your racecar go! You can rewind it and run it over and over again. Be careful with the long brass tube because it will bend. You can easily straighten it by hand, but it will eventually become too weak to stay straight. Bending the bar slightly to each side can also help the car stay straight. Experiment and have fun.

Additional Racecar Topics

The length of the lever arm on the spring hammer controls how many times the wheels spin. More spins equal more distance.

HAULING CHEESE

This racer is designed to set speed records.

Adult supervision required

Rolling Gear

Mousetrap

Needle-nose pliers

2 screw eyes (or straw)

1 short piece of balsa wood, 2 inches by 6 inches

2 long pieces of balsa wood, 1 inch by 12 inches

Glue

Drill and bits

Wire hangers (for metal axles)

High density foam wheels (from hobby store)

Duct tape or masking tape

Fishing line or thread

Step 1: Use the pliers to remove the hold-down wire and bait platform from a mousetrap to save weight.

Step 2: Unhook the hammer wire by pulling it to the side of the mousetrap.

Step 3: Use the pliers to straighten out the hammer wire.

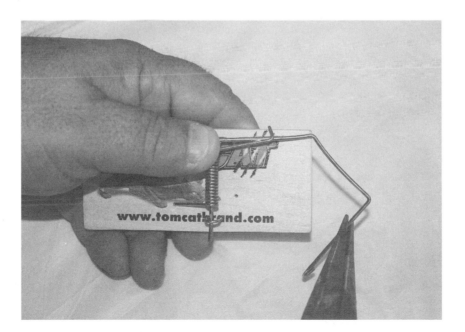

Step 4: Bend the hammer wire so that the hook is in line with the center of the mousetrap.

Step 5: Put 2 screw eyes in the front edge of a 2-inch-by-6-inch piece of balsa wood.

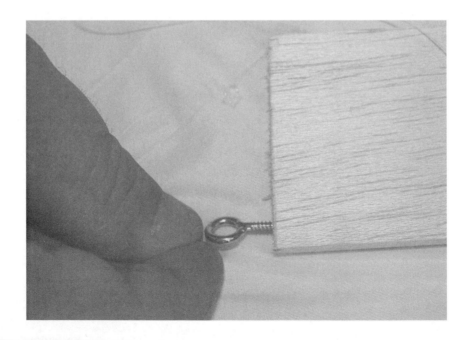

Step 6: Glue the mousetrap to the top of the short, 2-inch-by-6-inch piece of balsa wood, about a ½ inch from the back (the screw eyes are the front). Then glue the edges of this assembly between the two long, 1-inch-by-12-inch strips of balsa wood. Line up the front edge of the mousetrap piece with the front edge of the long strips. You can use superglue (with adult permission) to speed up the drying time. If you use wood glue, allow at least 6 hours to dry.

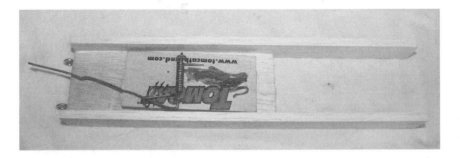

Step 7: Have an adult drill a hole at the back end of both long side pieces. The axle should spin freely in the holes.

Step 8: Cut axles from a wire hanger, or buy metal axles from a hobby store. Slide one wheel onto a metal axle. Slide the axle through the holes you just drilled and then slide the other wheel onto the other end. Foam tires will give you great traction and are available at hobby stores. You can also take wheels off an old remote control car.

Step 9: Wrap a 1-inch-by-12-inch strip of duct tape (or masking tape) around the rear axle.

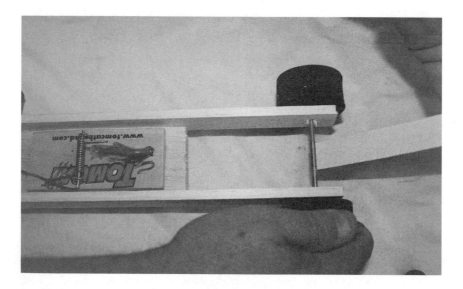

Step 10: The completed rear axle should look like this photo. It may take some testing to determine the ideal thickness for this tape roll for your individual car.

Step 11: Tie one end of your fishing line or thread around the tape roll and secure the knot with a small piece of tape.

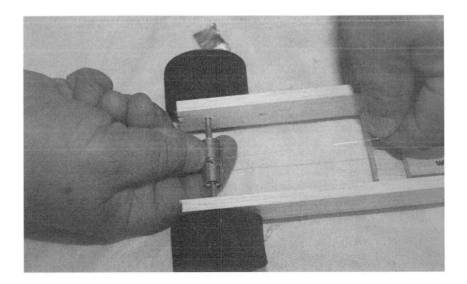

Step 12: Secure the other end of the fishing line or thread to the end of the hammer using a knot and tape.

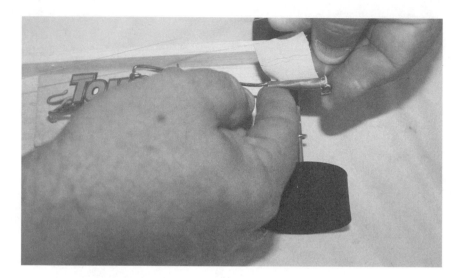

Step 13: Pull the hammer back with one hand as you spin the rear wheels to wind the string around the rear axle. You are now ready to put the racecar down and let it roll.

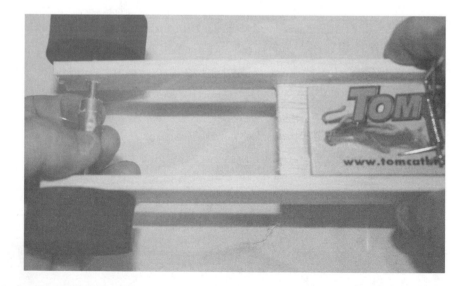

Additional Racecar Topics

This car is built for speed. To minimize friction with the wheels, you can try a few things. Putting two metal washers between the wood sides and the wheels will decrease friction. You can also drill out the center of the wheels and use small ball bearings that can be found at hobby stores. Less friction when the wheels are turning increases your speed.

THE BIG CHEESE

The Big Cheese lives up to its name. It is capable of setting distance records.

Adult supervision required

Rolling Gear

2 yardsticks

Drill and bits

2 pieces of balsa wood, 2 inches by 6 inches

Wood glue or superglue

Small wooden dowel

4 foam disks (from the floral department)

Hot glue

36-inch-long dowel

Pocketknife (or sandpaper)

Mousetrap

Duct tape

Fishing line or thread

Pliers

Step 1: Stack two yardsticks and, with adult help, drill holes through both yardsticks about 1 inch from the end at each end. The bit size should be slightly larger than the small dowel size. You will use the small dowel for axles.

Step 2: Glue the long edge of a 2-inch-by-6-inch piece of balsa wood to one of the yardsticks about 2 inches from the end—one inch past the hole, so it doesn't interfere with the axle.

Step 3: Put glue on the other 6-inch edge of the balsa wood. Place the other yardstick on top. Slide a piece of the axle dowel into the holes as you glue the yardstick in place to keep the holes aligned. Let the glue dry completely. Superglue is faster than wood glue, but you will need adult help or supervision to use it.

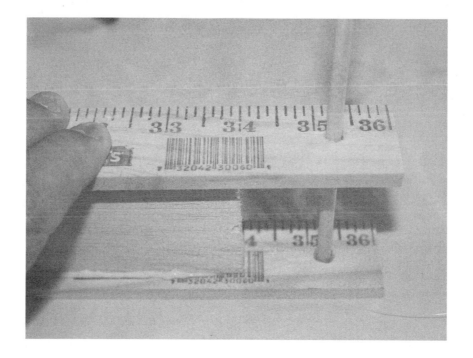

Step 4: Cut the small dowel to be 1 inch longer than the finished width of the car's body. Find the center of each foam disk and twist the dowel to create a divot in the foam. Do not push all the way through the disk.

Step 5: Fill the divot you just created in one foam disk with hot glue and immediately put the axle in. Fill up the hole in another foam disk with hot glue. Slide the axle through both yardsticks and attach the other disk. Make sure the wheels are parallel to each other and perfectly vertical, straight up and down. Repeat for the other axle and wheels. If you have any metal washers, you can put them between the yardsticks and wheels to help reduce friction.

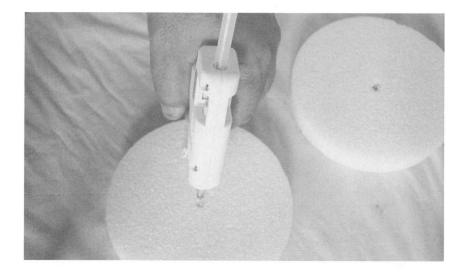

Step 6: Use pliers to remove the hold down wire and the bait platform of the mousetrap. It is easier to attach the dowel before attaching the mousetrap. Shave down one end of the 36-inch dowel to a V. You can use a knife (with adult help) or sandpaper. The V makes it fit under the spring of the mousetrap. Lay a 6-inch-long piece of duct tape under the hammer wire with the sticky side up. Slide the dowel into the center of the hammer wire. Once the dowel is centered, wrap the tape tightly around the dowel to hold it in place. Press the tape down as tightly as possible. You can add more tape if desired.

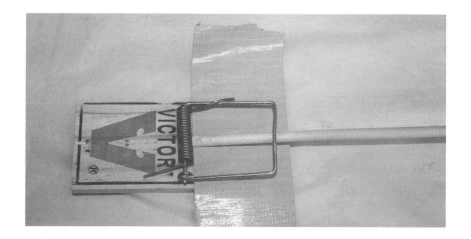

Step 7: Use wood glue or superglue to attach the mousetrap to one of the blocks of wood. When the spring is relaxed, the dowel should extend away from the middle of the car. Secure a 6-foot-long piece of fishing line or thread to the end of the dowel using a knot and tape. Leave the other end untied. Wrap this loose end around the rear axle as you pull back on the long dowel. Friction from the string and rear axle will hold the fishing line or thread in place once you start spinning the rear axle to wind it up.

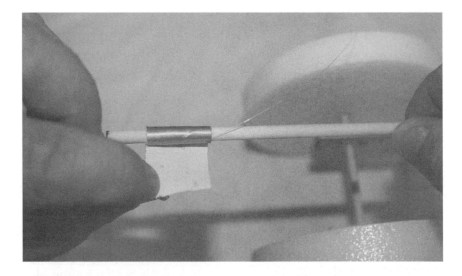

Step 8: Put the car down and watch it roll.

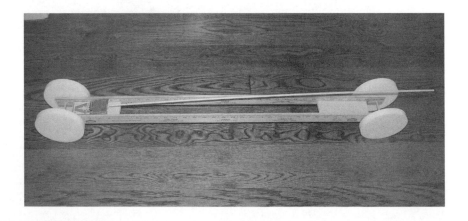

Additional Racecar Topics

This car makes a statement with its size. It also rolls well. You can add traction by putting rubber bands around the foam disk wheels. Adding weight to the rear block of wood may also help the car's traction. You can experiment with the weight needed since it can rest on the rear wood block. Try fishing weights or coins to see if you can increase your distance.

Mousetrap Car Kits and Websites

Mousetrap cars are a science competition staple, and a number of commercial kits are available for purchase. The commercially available kits usually include wheels, axles, bodies, and a mousetrap. They eliminate the need for cutting and drilling. Kits are available at most hobby stores and over the Internet.

The widest choices of kits come from Doc Fizzix (www.docfizzix.com). The basic level Doc Fizzix kits are found at hobby stores, and the website is a treasure trove for budding mousetrap car builders. The website is packed with useful information on how to tweak your car and is certainly the most comprehensive mousetrap car website on the Internet.

Another great source for low-cost mousetrap car kits is www.kelvin.com, an educational supply house of science stuff. Just search for mousetrap cars and see what they have. Kelvin offers gear-driven and pulley-driven mousetrap car kits. It also offers rubber band–powered car kits and air-powered car kits.

Just put mousetrap cars into any search engine and dozens of websites may lead you to new ideas for how to build a better mousetrap car.

3
Rubber Band Racers

Build and launch these fun rollers that get all their power from rubber bands. When rubber bands are stretched or wound up, they store elastic potential energy. This energy comes from you as you stretch or wind them. The energy stored in the bands is just waiting to come out and launch your cool toys across the ground.

SPOOL RACER

Here's a simple design to race across your kitchen floor.

Rolling Gear

Paper clip	2 toothpicks
Rubber band	Tape
Thread spool (can be empty or full)	Bead, washer, or Cheerio

Step 1: Straighten out a paper clip, but leave the hook on the larger end. Double up a small rubber band and place it on the hook.

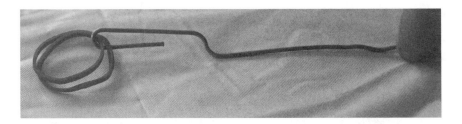

Step 2: Push the straight end of the paper clip through the center of the spool and grab the straight end as it comes out the other side.

Step 3: Break a toothpick in half. Insert the broken end through both loops of the rubber band and pull the straight end of the paper clip so that the toothpick is held in place against the spool.

Step 4: Place a small piece of tape over the broken toothpick to keep it from spinning.

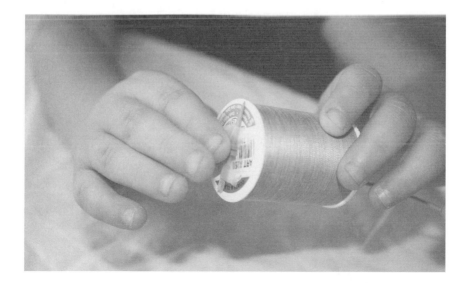

Step 5: Slide a plastic bead over the straight end of the paper clip and slide it down over the two ends of the hook of the paper clip. You can use a washer or even a Cheerio in place of the bead. You may have to bend the loop of the paper clip tighter depending on the opening in the bead, washer, or Cheerio.

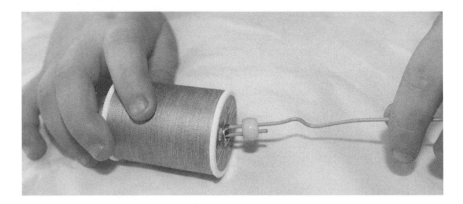

Step 6: Pull on the paper clip and slide the bead all the way to the spool, onto the rubber band. This is to lessen the friction and make the rubber band spin more easily.

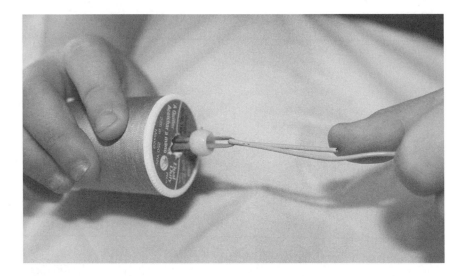

Step 7: Slide a full toothpick through both loops of the rubber band. The toothpick needs to be *outside* the bead to lessen friction. Unhook the paper clip hook from the rubber band.

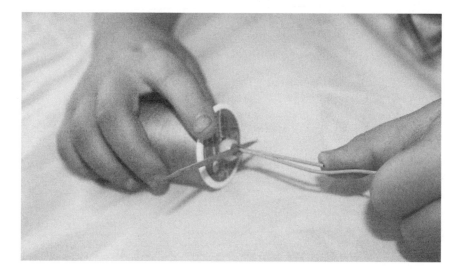

Step 8: Hold the spool in one hand and wind up the rubber band using the long toothpick.

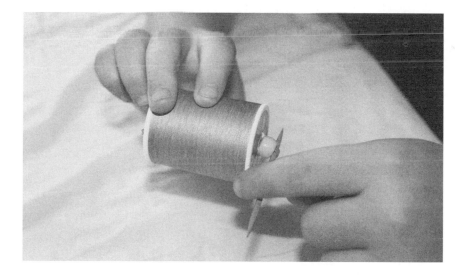

Step 9: Put the Spool Racer on the tabletop and let it go.

Additional Racecar Topics

Energy comes from the wound-up rubber band. Try winding it more and see what happens. Be careful not to wind it so tightly that you break the rubber band. However, if it is twisted tightly enough (and doesn't break), the Spool Racer will even stand up and do a little dance for you.

CHIP CAN DANCER

An empty Pringles can and a rubber band power this car to long distance records.

Adult supervision required

Rolling Gear

Bamboo skewer

Pringles can

Sharp knife, scissors, or drill

File folder rubber band (much longer than a
normal rubber band)

Paper clip

Small jewelry bead or washer (optional)

Step 1: Break a bamboo skewer with your bare hands. You need two pieces; one that is 2 inches long and the remaining longer piece.

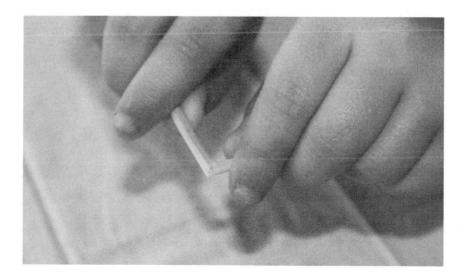

Step 2: This step will require adult help. You need to create holes in the center of the metal bottom and the plastic top of your Pringles can. An adult can use a drill, but since the metal is very thin, the hole can also be created in other ways. The sharp point of a steak knife or scissors will work. Put the point against the center of the metal bottom. Carefully grasp the dull edge of the blade and rotate it like a drill. Once the hole is created, continue to rotate until you have made a hole about the size of a pencil eraser. Repeat for the plastic top.

Step 3: Push a file folder rubber band through the hole in the metal bottom. File folder rubber bands are designed for businesses to put around giant file folders. They are available in all office supply stores and big box retail stores in the office supply section.

Step 4: Slide the smaller piece of bamboo skewer through the rubber band.

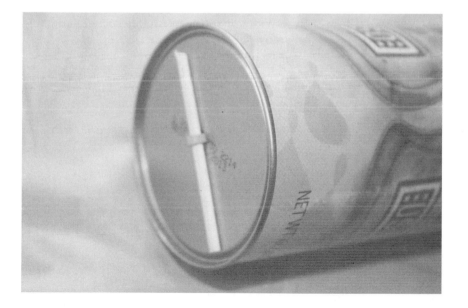

Step 5: Open up a paper clip by bending out the inner loop until it makes an S shape with the outer loop. Insert the smaller loop through the hole in the plastic top.

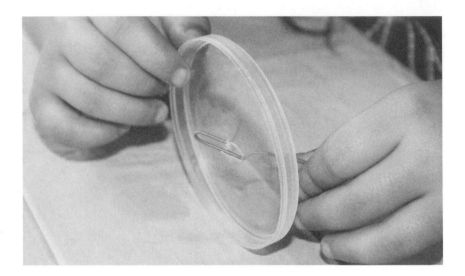

Step 6: Hook the smaller loop of the paper clip to the rubber band. You can probably reach up into the can to grab the other end of the rubber band. Make sure the plastic top is facing the right way so it can close onto the can.

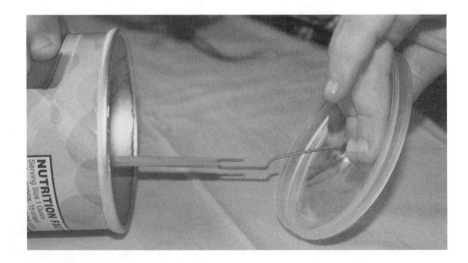

Step 7: Pull on the big loop of the paper clip so that the rubber band comes through the cover. Slide the longer bamboo skewer piece through the rubber band. You want the broken end to go through the rubber band. For really great results, slide the rubber band through a small jewelry bead before hooking it on the bamboo skewer. A washer or two, if available, between the cover and the bamboo skewer will also help it roll better.

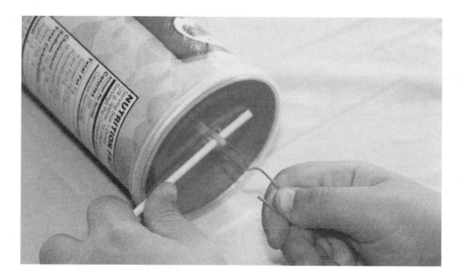

Step 8: Hold the can in one hand and use your finger to wind up the rubber band by turning the bamboo skewer. You will need to wind it 50 to 100 times to store enough elastic potential energy in the rubber band. Be careful you don't wind it too much. If it's too tight, the can won't roll.

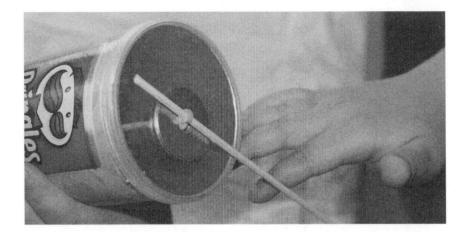

Step 9: After the rubber band is wound tight, pull on the long skewer part so that a few wound-up knots in the rubber band are outside the plastic top. This will make the Chip Can Dancer roll more easily.

Step 10: Put the Chip Can Dancer down on the floor and let it roll on.

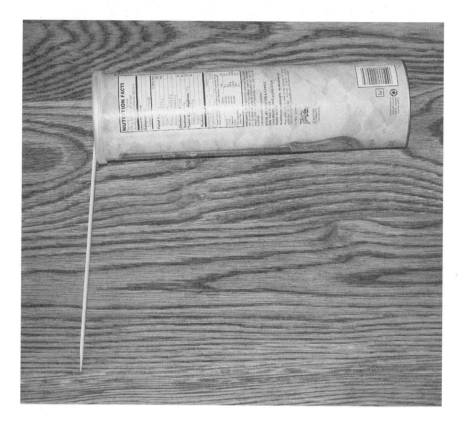

Additional Racecar Topics

The elastic potential energy of the rubber band is what makes the Chip Can Dancer go. Experiment with how many turns give you the best distance. Winding it too tightly causes too much friction with the long skewer and the top of the Pringles can. Build two and challenge a friend to a "roll-off" championship.

FOAM RACER

Turn old packing foam into a room-racing foam car.

Adult supervision required

Rolling Gear

Packaging foam

Sharp knife

3 round floral foam disks, 6 inches in diameter

1 or 2 bamboo skewers

Scissors

Hot glue

Rubber band

Paper clip

Tape

Step 1: You will need to use a sharp knife for this part, so get adult help and permission. A serrated knife works the best on foam.

Almost all electronics your family buys will be packed with foam spacers to hold the items during shipping. Take a look at the pieces to see which single piece would work best for the body of your racer. You will need to cut a skinny U at one end of the racer and a fatter U at the other end. You might find a piece that already has one of those done for you.

The rear, fatter U cut needs to be at least 3 inches wide and 2 inches long. Leave enough on either side to securely hold the rear axle.

For the skinny, front U cut, you need to have the foam disks in hand before you make the cut. Foam disks make great wheels. They are sold in stores that sell artificial flowers—dollar stores, craft stores, and big box stores. The disks are used in vases to hold the fake flowers in place. Cut the skinny U only slightly wider than the foam wheel. The length must be greater than half the diameter of the foam wheel.

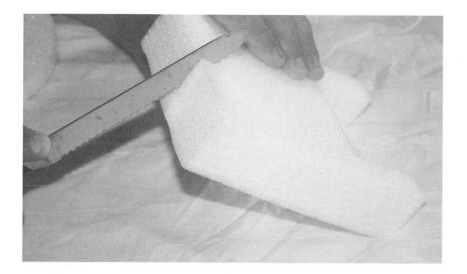

Step 2: Cut a bamboo skewer 1 inch longer than the width of your foam racecar body for the rear axle. Keep the other piece for the front axle, if long enough.

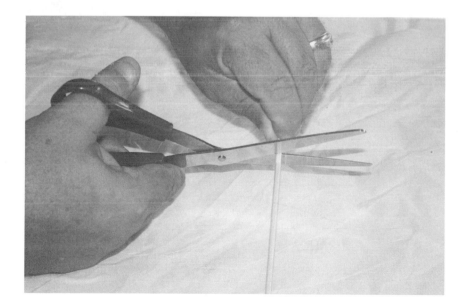

Step 3: Slide the pointed end of the skewer through the sides of the fat U, near the back of the foam body. It needs to be in the middle of the fat U. Wiggle the skewer around to widen the hole. This back axle needs to spin freely in the foam. Pull the skewer out after creating the holes.

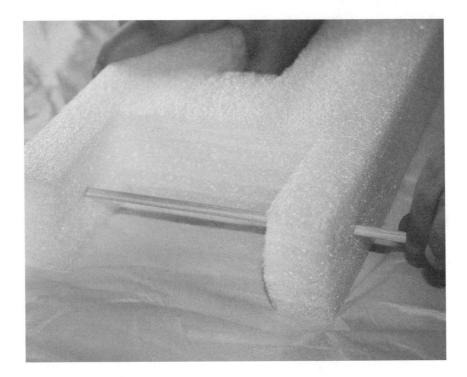

Step 4: Push one end of the cut skewer into the center of one foam disk about halfway to create a divot, and pull it out. Push the skewer into the center of the other wheel halfway and leave it there.

Step 5: Use hot glue to hold the axle in place. Always get permission or adult help to use a hot glue gun.

Step 6: After the glue dries, slide the axle through the hole you made in the rear of the Foam Racer.

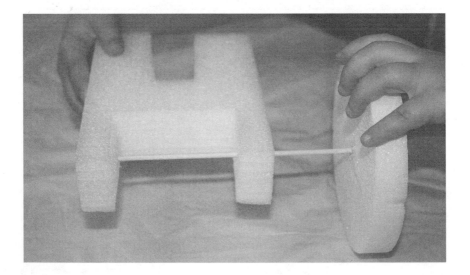

Step 7: Put hot glue in the center of the remaining rear wheel.

Step 8: Immediately put the other rear wheel onto the axle.

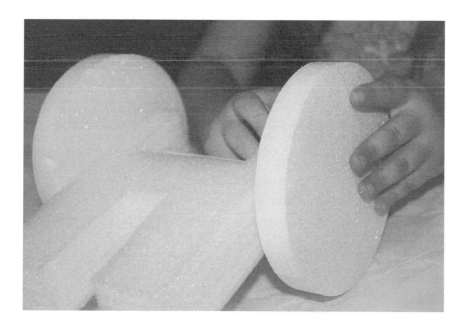

Step 9: Make sure the wheels are aligned straight up and down. Leave about a ¼-inch gap between the wheel and the car body to allow the wheels to roll freely. Let the racer sit for a few minutes to allow the hot glue to dry.

Step 10: Push a skewer all the way through the remaining wheel. Wiggle the skewer around to widen this hole, and then pull the skewer out. Unlike the rear wheels, this wheel will spin freely around a fixed axle, so the hole needs to be slightly larger than the axle's diameter.

Step 11: Slide the remaining skewer piece through one side of the skinny U. You may have to cut another skewer depending on the width of your Foam Racer.

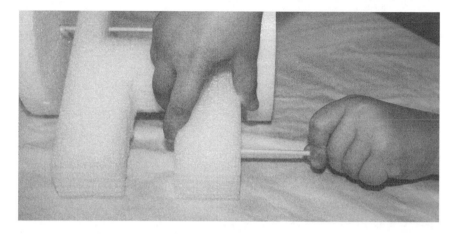

Step 12: Place the front wheel in the skinny U. Slide the skewer through the center hole and into the other side of the skinny U. Make sure the front wheel spins easily.

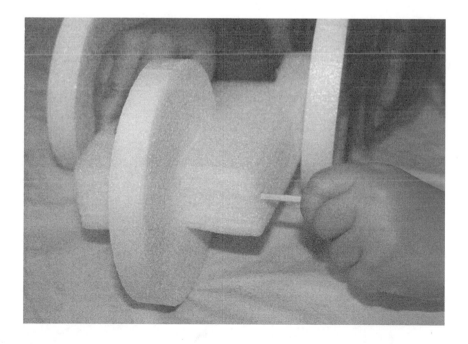

Step 13: Wrap a rubber band around the rear axle. Pull a loop of the rubber band through the band itself, as shown, to capture the rear axle.

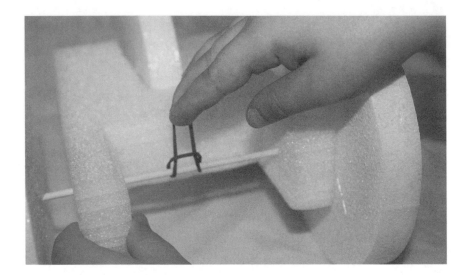

Step 14: Open a paper clip and bend it back and forth until it breaks, forming two U-shaped wires. You will use one loop of the clip to hold the end of the rubber band.

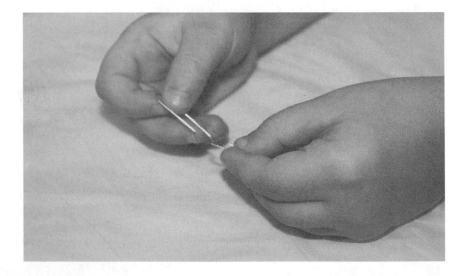

Step 15: Take the paper clip loop and capture the rubber band. Press the paper clip loop into the foam as shown.

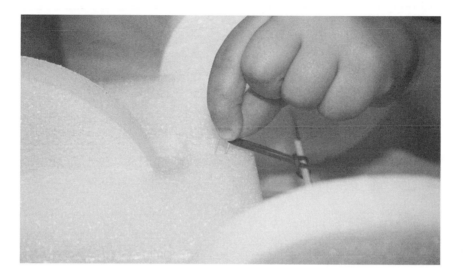

Step 16: Place a piece of tape over the rubber band on the rear axle to keep the rubber band from slipping.

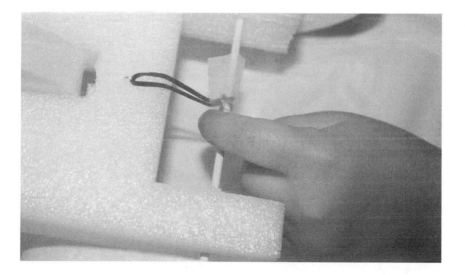

Step 17: Wind up the rear axle using your fingers. Wind the axle and not the wheels since the hot glue is not as strong as the axle. Hang on to the axle as shown until you are ready to race.

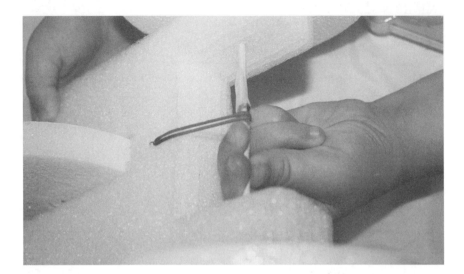

Step 18: Place the Foam Racer on the floor and let go of the axle.

Additional Racecar Topics

The elastic potential energy from the rubber band powers this lightweight racer. You can remove the rubber band easily and try another thicker or longer band. Try pieces of foam of different sizes. The wheels can be reused several times. Simply pull the wheels off the rear axle and add more hot glue. As always, get adult permission before you use a hot glue gun or a sharp knife.

ROLLING THUNDER

This cardboard-infused rolling machine is perfect for the great indoors.

Adult supervision required

Rolling Gear

Small peanut or Pringles can with pop-off lid	2 milk jug caps
Corrugated cardboard	Tape
Pen	2 pencils
Ruler	Screwdriver and hammer (or drill)
Sharp scissors	5 rubber bands
Bamboo skewer	Paper clip

Step 1: Lay the can on a piece of cardboard and make a mark ½ inch from the top and the bottom of the can. Make sure the corrugated part (long holes) run from the top of the can to the bottom of the can. Cut out a rectangle that is 3 inches wide and the length that you marked.

Step 2: Slide a bamboo skewer through the corrugated part of the cardboard. It doesn't matter if the skewer spins or not.

Step 3: Ask an adult to use the point of the scissors to make a hole in the center of both milk jug caps. A helpful hint is to hold the scissors and spin the cap. But be careful with the scissors!

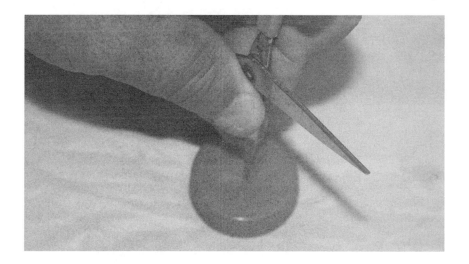

Step 4: Slide the milk jug caps onto the bamboo skewer to act as wheels. Wrap a piece of tape around the skewer just past the wheel, to keep the wheels from sliding off the skewer. The wheels should spin freely.

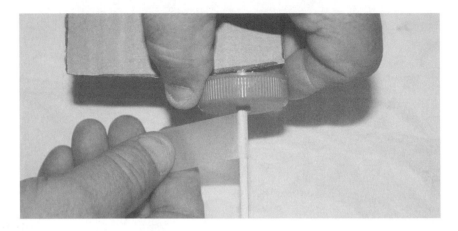

Step 5: Place two pencils on the cardboard rectangle near the edges. The space between the pencils should be slightly wider than the can. Line up the eraser ends along the line of the skewer axle. Secure the pencils with tape. Duct tape works best since it is extra strong, but any tape will work—you just might need more.

Step 6: Put the plastic pop-off lid on the bottom of the can. Make two marks with a pen about 1 inch apart.

Step 7: Get adult permission to use a hammer and screwdriver. Place the screwdriver on one of your marks. Hit the screwdriver with the hammer and make a hole in both the plastic top and the thin bottom of the can. Repeat for the other mark. You could also drill the holes if you have adult help.

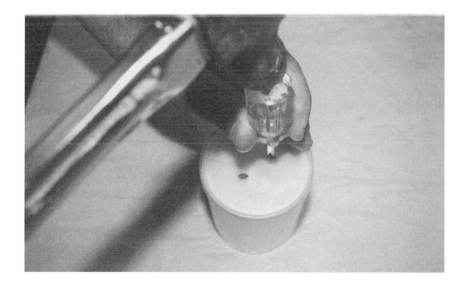

Step 8: Put three rubber bands around the middle of the can. Make sure they lie flat; the rubber will give you better traction.

Step 9: Put a medium-sized rubber band through each of the holes in the bottom of the can.

Step 10: Slide one of the pencils through both rubber bands and pull it tight to the can.

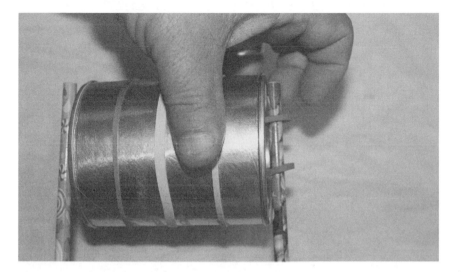

Step 11: Unfold a paper clip and make a long hook out of it. Hook one rubber band inside the can and then put the free end of the paper clip through the hole in the lid.

Step 12: Using the paper clip, pull the first rubber band through the hole in the plastic lid and secure the rubber band temporarily. You can use a toothpick, pen, or pencil to do this. Slide the paper clip out from underneath the rubber band.

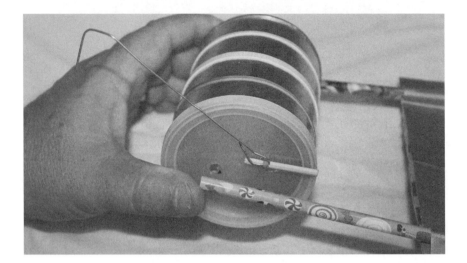

Step 13: Repeat Steps 11 and 12 for the other rubber band. After you remove the paper clip, you can pull on the rubber bands and slide the other pencil through.

Step 14: Spin the can to wind up the two rubber bands. You should spin the can in the direction opposite to how you want it to spin when released.

Step 15: Put the racer on a flat surface and let it go.

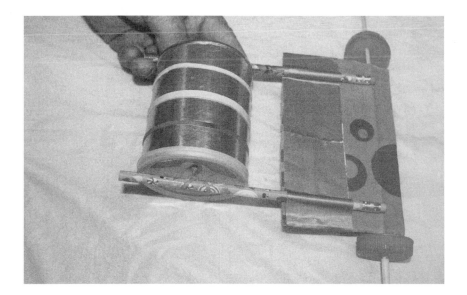

Additional Racecar Topics

Spin the can in the other direction to see which way Rolling Thunder moves. You can also slightly pop the lid and add pennies, marbles, or any small items to the inside of the can. This will help Rolling Thunder gain traction and will also add a little more thunder.

4-WHEELED FUN

Build this fun machine capable of rolling across the room.

Adult supervision required

Rolling Gear

3 flat foam panels (or cardboard), 6 inches by
12 inches

Sharp knife

4 old CDs

2 new pencils

4 small squares of cardboard

Hot glue

Rubber band

Duct tape

Step 1: Use a sharp knife to cut a U, about 3 inches wide by 4 inches long, out of the back of one foam panel, as shown. This panel will be the top of your car.

Note: Flat foam is found as packing material in boxes for electronics and assemble-it-yourself furniture. You can also use insulating foam panels found at home improvement stores. The same design could also be built using corrugated cardboard and duct tape instead of glue.

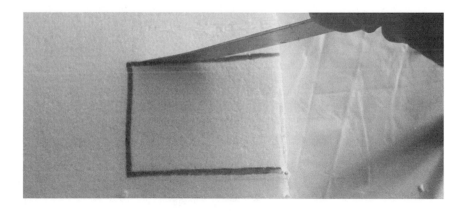

Step 2: Stack the other two foam panels. Place a CD near one corner and make sure the CD hangs over the bottom. Use a pencil to make a hole through both pieces of foam. Repeat at the other end, lengthwise. Be careful to make both axle holes at the same distance from the edge of the foam, and keep the pencil straight up and down. If you use cardboard, you will need to use a sharp knife to make the hole.

Step 3: After you have made the holes, use the pencil to expand them. The axle needs to spin freely. But don't overdo it or the car will wobble.

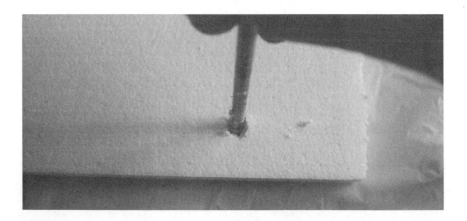

Step 4: Get adult help or permission to use a hot glue gun. Place a small cardboard square below the center CD hole. Stand the pencil perfectly straight up in the center of the hole. Add hot glue to hold the pencil in place. You will have to hold the pencil in place for a few minutes while the glue dries. The pencil must be perfectly vertical. Repeat for the other axle. Let both dry completely. You can work on Step 5 while the glue dries.

Step 5: Place a line of hot glue along the length of the top piece, near the edge. Stand a side piece on the line of hot glue and hold for 1 minute. Make sure the axle holes are away from the top piece. Repeat for the other side.

Step 6: Slide both CD wheel-axle combinations through the axle holes while the car is upside down.

Step 7: Lay another CD on top of a small piece of cardboard. Create a large puddle of hot glue directly in the center of the CD hole. Immediately pick up the CD and attach it to the other end of the axle. Make sure it is centered in the hole. Also make sure it is parallel to the side piece. You will have to hold it for about 2 minutes to let the hot glue completely harden.

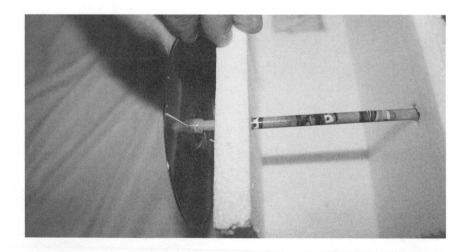

Step 8: Cut the rubber band to create a long rubber strip. Use a small piece of duct tape to tape it to the middle of the front axle, lined up with the middle of the U cut.

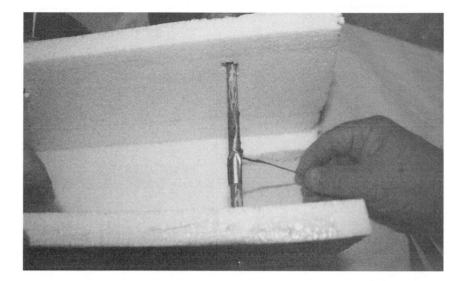

Step 9: Use a piece of duct tape to attach the other end to the top of the 4-Wheeled Fun racecar just behind the U cut.

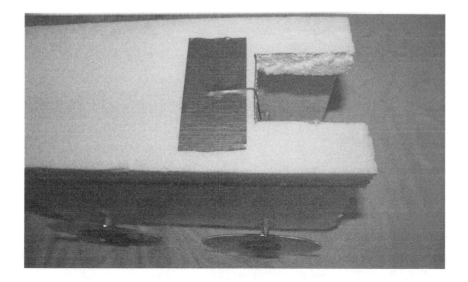

Step 10: Wind up the rubber band by spinning the pencil with your finger. Turn the car over, place it on the floor, and let it go.

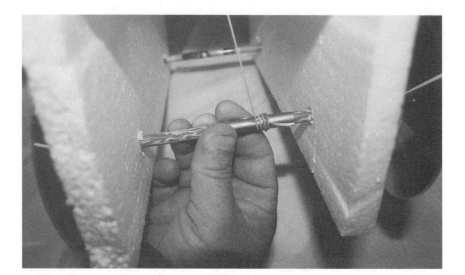

Additional Racecar Topics

Try different rubber bands to increase the racecar's distance. Cutting the rubber bands allows you to get more wheel turns, and more wheel turns equal more distance.

An advanced technique allows all rubber band–powered cars to freewheel (rolling without power) and potentially gain more distance. To get extra freewheel distance, do not attach the rubber band to the axle. You will need to hold it in place with one hand as you wind up the axle. After a few turns, friction between the rubber band and the axle will hold it in place. Wind up the car and let it go. You will usually get more distance.

If the rubber band is attached, it will unwind all of its turns. When unwound completely and while the car is rolling, the rubber band will start to wind up on the axle the other way. This will cause the car to slow down and maybe even roll back to you. If the rubber band is unattached, this braking effect won't happen. But the loose rubber band may get tangled in the wheels, so experiment to find out what length and thickness of rubber band works the best. You can also use this same technique with the string on your mousetrap cars.

PROP CAR

Use the power of air to roll this car across the room.

Rolling Gear

Old toy car

Rubber band–powered airplane (can be broken)

Tape

Rubber band

Note: Rubber band–powered airplane kits are found at most toy stores, hobby stores, and old-fashioned general stores. These planes have been around for years. Your grandparents probably played with them as kids. Eventually the wings break, but all you really need for this project is the propeller and rubber band assembly.

Step 1: Find a suitable old toy that rolls well. Pictured is a broken sand truck for the beach, but any big-wheeled toy will work. You can also build your own base using Pringles can lids for wheels, bamboo skewers for axles, straws to hold the axles, and a ruler to act as the body.

Step 2: Place the center prop assembly of the airplane on top of the car. You can use tape or a small rubber band to hold it to the toy car. With the toy car pictured, the center assembly fit tightly between the seats.

Step 3: Place the long rubber band from the plane on the center strut. Wind up the rubber band and let it go.

Additional Racecar Topics

Try a number of different rubber bands and measure the distance. Try two rubber bands. The flight rubber bands are usually the same size as file rubber bands, which are sold anywhere they sell office supplies.

A great science fair project is to try the Prop Car on different surfaces to investigate friction. A few props can be spun the other way and actually push the car like an airboat.

4
Rocket Racers

All rockets use the principle of Newton's third law. By trapping gas into a confined area, you can store energy just like when you stretch a rubber band. The gas naturally wants to expand back to its original volume. Just think about blowing up a balloon. The trapped air is just dying to come out. And as it comes out, you can use it to power racecars. All rockets use the same principle. The escaping gas provides an action as it escapes, and creates a reaction that causes the rocket car to roll.

You can use a pump to increase the air pressure, or you can use a chemical reaction to create a gas. This gas will build up pressure until the rocket car launches. Either way, these racecars are fun (and occasionally messy). But it's all in the name of science.

BASIC AIR RACER

Modify an old toy to get it to roll across your dining room table.

Rolling Gear

Balloon
Straw
Scissors

Tape
Toy car

Step 1: First, blow up a balloon and let it deflate. After you stretch the rubber in a balloon, it becomes easier to do a second time. Cut a straw in half. Slide one half of the straw into the neck of the balloon. Twist the neck of the balloon to make it as airtight as possible.

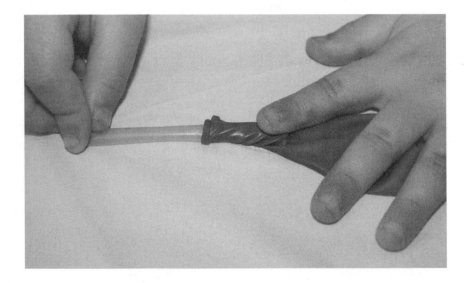

Step 2: Wrap a piece of tape around the neck of the balloon to secure the straw. You can test it by blowing up the balloon through the straw.

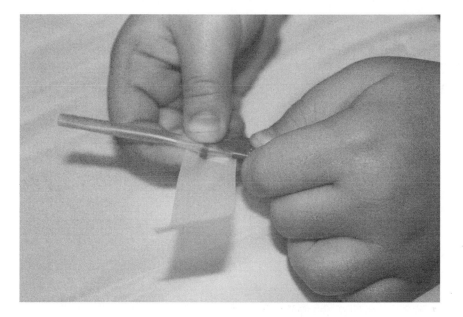

Step 3: Place the straw and balloon on top of a toy car with the balloon at the front and the straw pointing toward the back. Use a long piece of tape and attach the straw to the roof of the car. Be careful that the tape doesn't interfere with the wheels.

Step 4: Blow up the balloon through the straw. The best way to do this is to place both thumbs under the car and use your fingers to hold the straw in place. Be careful you don't pinch the straw closed. After you get the balloon inflated, use your thumb or finger to seal the end of the straw.

Step 5: Place the car on a flat, smooth surface, release the straw, and watch the car race.

Additional Racecar Topics

Try different cars and different surfaces. You can even try different size balloons.

MINI POP CAR

Use a fizzy tablet to create a pop to launch your car.

Rolling Gear

Empty plastic film canister

Tape

Toy car

Water

Effervescent tablet

Note: Film canisters are getting harder to find as people switch to digital photography. Any photo processing place, like Walmart or most drug stores, will give you some if you ask. Empty pill containers will also work if they have a pop-off lid.

Step 1: Tape an empty film canister to the top of a Hot Wheel–sized toy car. Face the open top of the canister toward the rear of the car.

Step 2: Find a flat, smooth surface outside. The area under the car will get wet, so driveways and sidewalks are perfect. Aiming down an inclined driveway will also help the Mini Pop Car go farther. Remove the film canister cap and pour about half an inch of water into the canister.

Step 3: Place an effervescent tablet on the inside of the cap so that when you close and seal the canister, the tablet will be inside. Effervescent tablets are any Alka-Seltzer–type tablets. Store brand tablets work just as well as more expensive brands for this racecar.

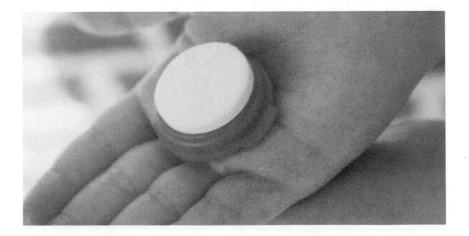

Step 4: Be sure to aim the cap away from any person as you do this step. Snap the cap down onto the canister and **immediately** place on the driveway. Move away and stand to the side of the Mini Pop Car. It will pop as it launches. The car won't go far, but the top will really fly. You may be able to reuse the tablet if it pops out; each tablet should give you at least two pops.

Additional Racecar Topics

A chemical reaction creates the gas, which builds up the pressure. When the pressure is high enough, the cap pops off. The top flying off causes the car to roll. Of course, the top goes much farther than the car because of its lighter weight. But the startling pop makes it worth doing anyway. You can try lighter cars and different amounts of water.

POP BOTTLE RACECAR

Use a bicycle pump to shoot this rocket car to the end of the driveway.

Adult supervision required

Rolling Gear

Corrugated cardboard

Scissors

Old set of wheels with axles

Tape

Empty drink bottle

Drill and bits

Tire valve

Rubber stopper or cork

Bicycle pump

Step 1: Cut a 2-inch-by-8-inch rectangle from a scrap piece of corrugated cardboard. The size may need to vary based on your bottle size and wheel types.

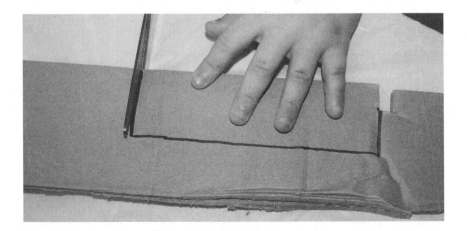

Step 2: You can use an old set of wheels from a medium-sized broken toy car. Take the toy car apart and salvage the wheels and axles. (You might want to hang on to the

other parts for use on other racecar projects.) Slide an axle with a wheel on one side through the corrugated part of the cardboard at one end. Slide the other wheel back on the other side of the axle. Repeat for the rear of the cardboard piece. You can also use any type of wheel and a nail for the axle if you don't have an old broken toy.

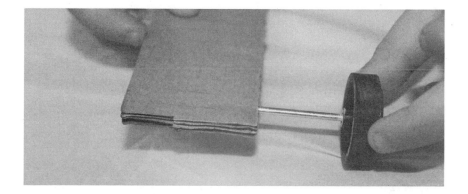

Step 3: Take a 10-inch piece of tape and wrap it partly around the flat label area of your drink bottle. The picture shows duct tape, but any tape will work. If you use thin clear tape, you might need two strips.

Step 4: Wrap the tape around the cardboard. Make sure the wheels can roll freely and the car will roll when placed on the ground.

Step 5: With adult help, pick out a drill bit that matches the size of your tire valve. An old bike tire valve is shown, but a ball inflation needle will also work.

Step 6: With adult help, drill a hole through the middle of your rubber stopper. A cork will also work. The stopper or cork must fit tightly in the neck of your Pop Bottle Racecar.

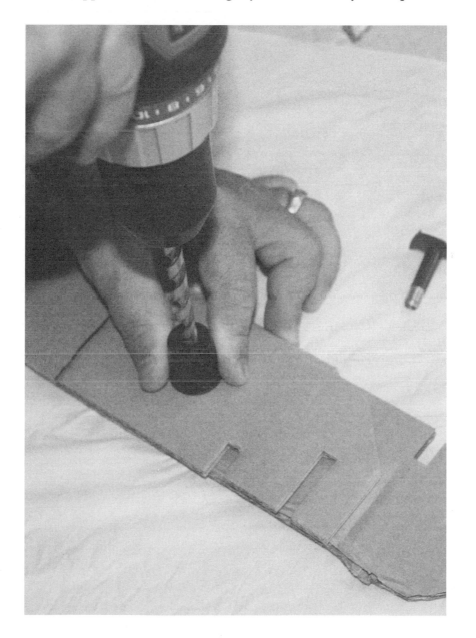

Step 7: Push the valve through the stopper so that the brass end comes out of the wide end of the stopper.

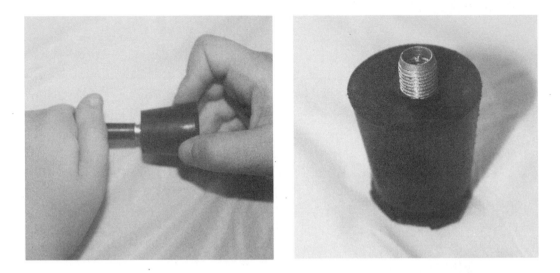

Step 8: Push the stopper into the neck of your Pop Bottle Racecar.

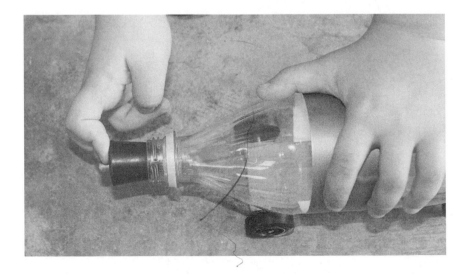

Step 9: The weight of the tire pump valve may cause your car to do a wheelie. That is OK. Attach the bicyle pump to the pump vale and pump the bicycle pump as hard as you can. When the air pressure inside the bottle is high enough, your racecar will pop off and race.

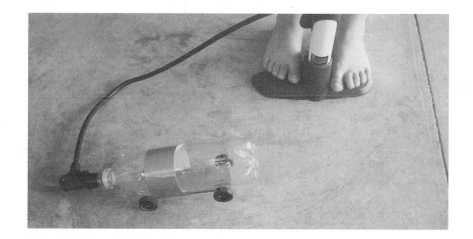

Additional Racecar Topics

Your Pop Bottle Racecar works because of air pressure. When the force supplied by the air pressure is greater than the friction between the stopper and the neck, the car pops off. You can vary how tightly you push in the stopper. You can also try different size bottles by simply cutting the tape and using a new bottle.

MINI BALLOON RACECAR

Rolling Gear

Cardboard

Pen

Small circular object

Scissors

Straw

Tape

Balloon

2 bamboo skewers

Step 1: Trace around a small (about 2-inch) jar lid or other circular object on a scrap piece of corrugated cardboard. Trace 4 circles.

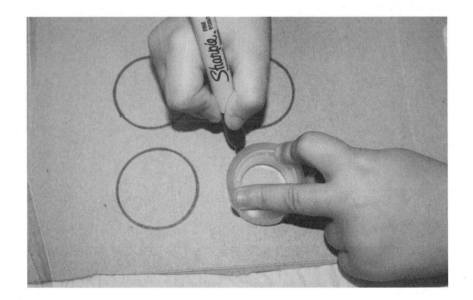

Step 2: Use scissors to cut out the wheels. Cut along the outside of the line to keep the wheels perfectly circular. Cutting the cardboard into 4 smaller sections before the final trim may be helpful.

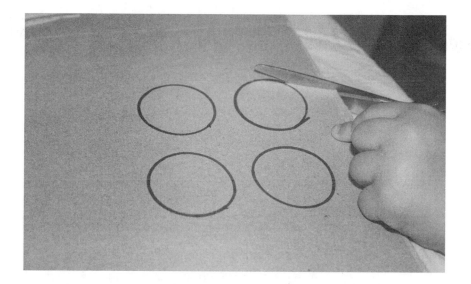

Step 3: Use the point of the scissors to create a tiny hole in the center of each wheel. Unfold the scissors and spin the point into the cardboard. Use a piece of scrap cardboard under the wheel to avoid marking the table underneath.

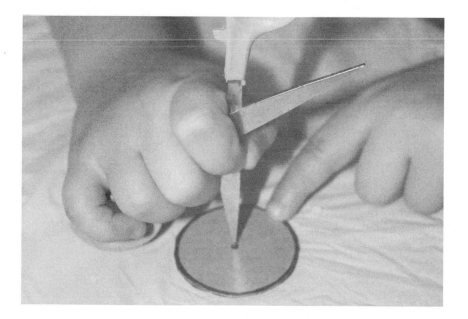

Step 4: Cut out a 3-inch-by-4-inch piece of cardboard. It is easiest to cut along one corner of the cardboard for at least one side. The dimensions can vary slightly based on your cardboard piece.

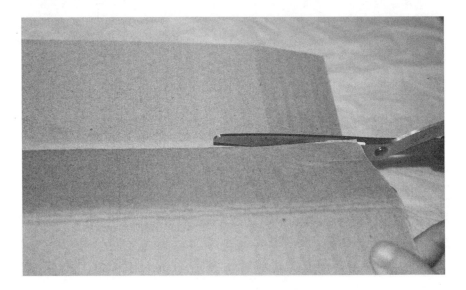

Step 5: Cut two pieces of straw slightly wider than the short side of the car base.

Step 6: Tape two pieces of a drinking straw across the front bottom and rear bottom of your car base.

Step 7: Blow up a balloon and let it deflate four or five times. Stretching the rubber makes it easier to blow up each time. Insert a 6-inch piece of straw into the balloon neck. Wrap tape around the neck to seal the balloon. You should be able to blow up the balloon through the straw without air slipping out.

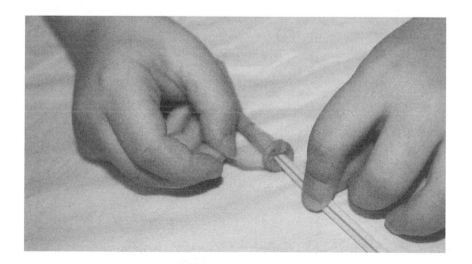

Step 8: Insert the pointed end of a bamboo skewer through the small hole in the center of the wheel. Slide the first wheel over about 4 inches.

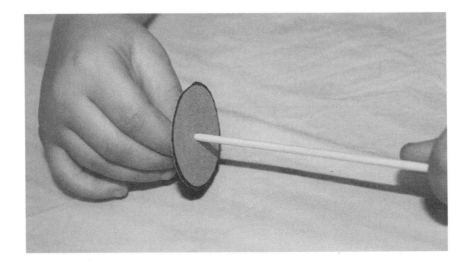

Step 9: Slide the pointed end through one straw on the base of your car. Slide another wheel onto the pointed end. It helps to twist the skewer as you do this.

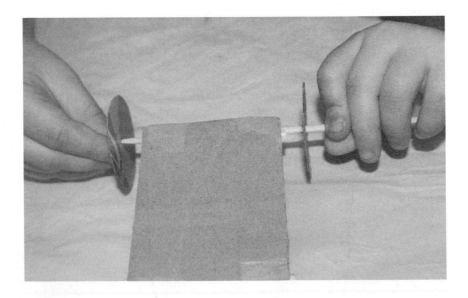

Step 10: Use the scissors to cut the skewer about ½ inch outside of the wheel. The scissors will probably just score the skewer, but it will break easily at that score.

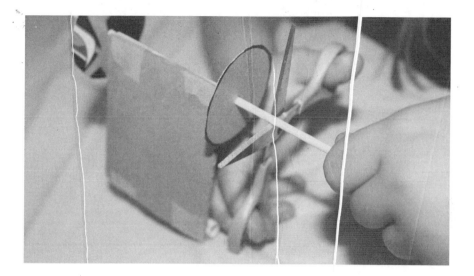

Step 11: Repeat for the pointed end of the skewer. Repeat Steps 8 through 11 for the other wheel-axle combination.

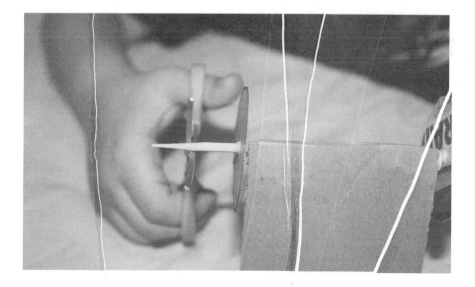

Step 12: Tape the neck of the balloon to the cardboard base. Make sure you let the straw hang over the end and beyond the wheels. This makes it easier to inflate.

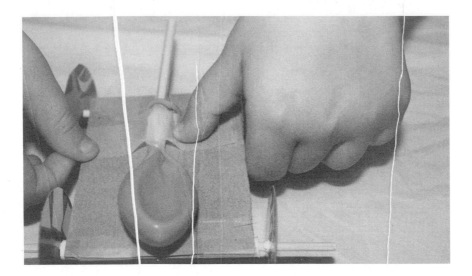

Step 13: Your Mini Balloon Racecar is ready to race. Blow up the balloon through the straw and pinch the straw closed. Set the car on the ground, release the straw, and let it ride.

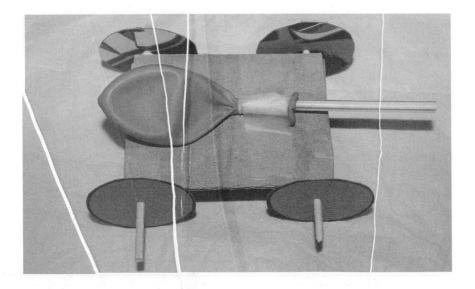

Additional Racecar Topics

The Mini Balloon Racecar works because of Isaac Newton's third law of motion: for every action, there is an equal and opposite reaction. The air rushing out is the action and the car rolling in the opposite direction is the reaction. Also, watch the car really speed up as it loses air because it is getting lighter. Try different size and shape balloons to see which works best.

VINEGAR RACER

Use baking soda and vinegar to launch this car down the sidewalk.

Rolling Gear

Set of wheels

Piece of wood

Nails

Hammer

Small empty drink bottle with pop-up top

Tape

Aluminum foil

Thick pen

Paper

Baking soda

Measuring spoon

Vinegar

Step 1: Put the wheels on the scrap piece of wood. Pictured is a pinewood derby kit available at all craft and hobby stores. Put on all four wheels and test roll the car. It should roll easily. You could use any old toy wheels and a scrap piece of wood.

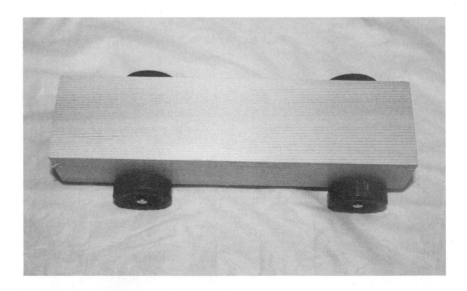

Step 2: Tape the empty drink bottle to the wooden base. The top of the bottle should extend slightly beyond the end of the base.

Step 3: Take a 3-inch square of aluminum foil and lay a thick pen on top.

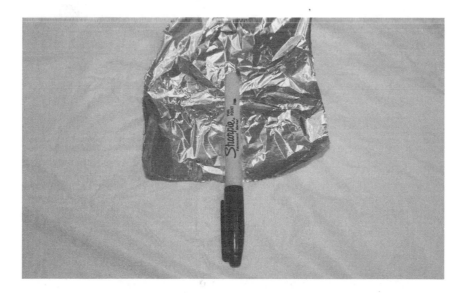

Step 4: Fold the bottom up and then roll the aluminum foil around the pen. Remove the pen from the aluminum foil, being careful not to crush the tube.

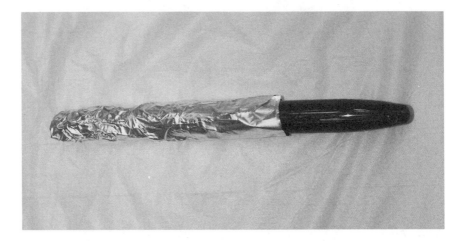

Step 5: Fold and crease a piece of paper. Place 1 tablespoon of baking soda in the middle of the paper.

Step 6: Go outside to do the rest of the steps, as it will make cleanup much easier. Pick the paper up and pour the baking soda into the aluminum foil tube.

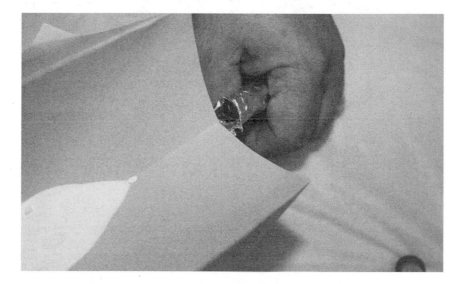

Step 7: Pour vinegar into the bottle. Fill it about ⅔ of the way full.

Step 8: Slide the aluminum foil tube into the mouth of the bottle.

Step 9: Put the top on and make sure the pop-up top is pressed down.

Step 10: Shake the car as you lay it down and immediately pop the top.

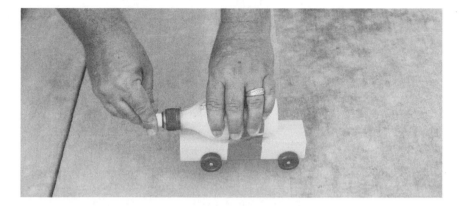

Step 11: Watch out for the spray as your Vinegar Racer goes rolling down the sidewalk.

Additional Racecar Topics

Combining baking soda and vinegar creates carbon dioxide gas. As the gas is created the pressure builds. The carbon dioxide escaping out of the back propels the Vinegar Racer. You can vary the amounts of each ingredient to see which combination gives your Vinegar Racer the highest speed.

COLA ROLLER

Adult supervision required

Rolling Gear

Small screwdriver

Mentos mints

String

Straw

Scissors

Duct tape

Ruler

2 axles

4 wheels

Diet cola in plastic bottle

Drill and bits

Step 1: With a small screwdriver, make a hole in the center of a Mentos mint. You could also use a drill bit. The bit does not need to be mounted in the drill. Repeat for three mints.

Step 2: Slide a piece of string through the holes in the mints and tie a knot. Leave a long piece of string so you can pick up the mints with the string.

Step 3: Cut two 2-inch pieces of straw, and tape each one perpendicular to the ruler, one close to each end.

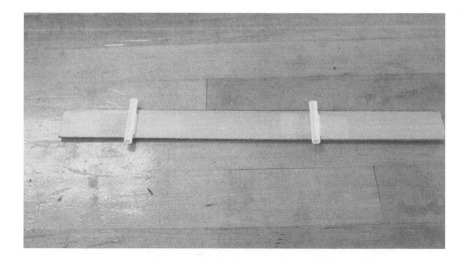

Step 4: Slide the axles through the straws and attach the wheels. Hobby store wheels were used here, but any wheel-axle combination will work.

Step 5: Take the top off the bottle of diet cola and keep the bottle upright. With adult help, drill a small hole in the cap of the bottle.

Step 6: Let the end of the ruler rest on the table and use duct tape to tape the bottle to the ruler.

Step 7: Do this and the next step outside, on a driveway or sidewalk. Put the mints on the string through the hole in the cap. Pull up on the string so the mints are tight to the top as you put the cap on the bottle. **It is very important to keep the mints out of the cola until you are ready to set the car down.**

Step 8: Now you are ready to launch. Let go of the string and let the mints fall into the soda. Keep your thumb over the hole and shake the bottle once or twice. Keep clear of the back of the Cola Roller as you set it down or you will get wet . . . and sticky.

Additional Racecar Topics

Diet sodas work better than regular sodas. Many scientists think the large sugar molecules in regular sodas prevent the fast formation of bubbles. One thing is definite, it is easier to clean up the diet soda residue than sticky, sugary soda.

Carbon dioxide gas adds the carbonation to all sodas. Normally, the carbonation will come out as you drink it over time. Mentos mints have a rough surface, and the rough surface allows thousands of bubbles of gas to be created at once. Each bubble adds to the pressure and pushes the gas and soda mixture out the hole in the top. The action of the mixture leaving the bottle causes a reaction and the Cola Roller rolls. Try different size sodas and different types of sodas. You can even try a 2-liter bottle on a skateboard for a giant rocket racer.

5
Edible Racers

Building rolling machines is fun. Building rolling machines you can eat is even better. Veggies, fruits, candy, crackers, and cookies can all be used to build racecars. Be creative with your design. Science can be fun *and* tasty.

Edible racecar contests are enjoyable for all ages and are very popular in elementary and middle schools. There are two types of contests: long distance roll and beauty. Either contest would be great for class projects, scouting troops, vacation bible schools, and the like.

A long distance roll contest will need a starting ramp. The car that rolls farthest from the bottom of the ramp wins. A good angle for the ramp is 30 degrees. Ramps can be made from wood or cardboard. Any flat substance will do. Have enough angle on the ramp that the cars get some speed before they reach the bottom.

For an edible car beauty contest, you need impartial judges. Judging could be based on color, creativity, or perhaps even nutritional value, in which case veggie cars get higher scores that candy cars.

If you are going to have a contest, set the rules for car construction based on what is best for you. Do you want cars that are 100 percent edible? In that case, spaghetti noodles make decent axles (but are fragile). Many edible car contests allow some nonfood items, such as toothpicks. If someone else set the rules, be sure you abide by all of them.

All edible cars need several things: axles, wheels, hubs, and bodies. Good axles need to be strong and straight. The following are a few good choices:

- Pretzel sticks or rods
- Toothpicks
- Bamboo skewers
- Spaghetti noodles
- Penne noodles

Good wheels need to be round and need a hole at the center. You can create your own holes in softer foods. Any round food will do, but here are a few ideas:

- Round cereals
- Round cookies
- Apple slices
- Potato slices
- Cucumber slices
- Wagon wheel pasta
- Mini donuts

Hubs are designed to keep the wheels on the axles. Lug nuts on a car wheel serve this purpose. You might use tape or glue to act as a hub on other racecars, but edible cars need edible hubs. You need something smaller than your wheel that can hold the wheel on. Here are a few good choices:

- Raisins
- Craisins
- Jelly beans
- Soft fruit chews

One type of toothpick doesn't need a hub at all. Decorative toothpicks have plastic attached to one end. These are used in some restaurants to hold thick sandwiches together, but they are also available in the grocery store. However, the plastic can add some friction to the wheels so be aware of this when you design your racecar.

An edible car body needs to be soft enough that you can get axles into or through it, yet strong enough to roll down the ramp. Car bodies are usually longer than they are wide, but they don't have to be. Bodies also have to be strong enough to support the wheels and axles. Long, skinny snack cakes won't work; they just aren't strong enough. The following are a few good car body choices:

- Rolls or buns
- Cucumbers
- Potatoes
- Candy bars

Another option is to use a bamboo skewer to put several soft items together. The skewer will give you enough strength.

Use your creativity and science know-how to build the best racecar possible. Make sure you know the rules if it is a contest. But most of all, experiment and have fun. Add decorations and make the car fit your personality. Modify any of the designs you see here based on what you have in the kitchen.

MALLOW MAGIC

Use a few marshmallows to create a car that will roll across the table.

Rolling Gear

Bamboo skewers
Marshmallows
Penne or ziti pasta

Step 1: Push a bamboo skewer through the center of a marshmallow. Continue stacking until you have five or six marshmallows on the skewer. You can leave part of the skewer sticking out of the back for ease in steering and launching.

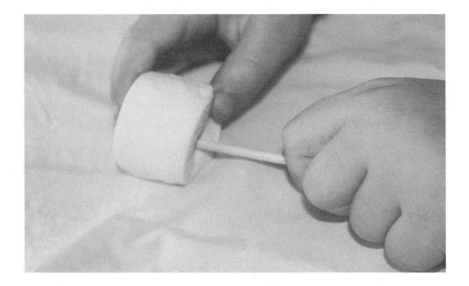

Step 2: Push an uncooked piece of penne pasta through each of the end marshmallows. Make sure you have both pasta pieces at the same height and angle.

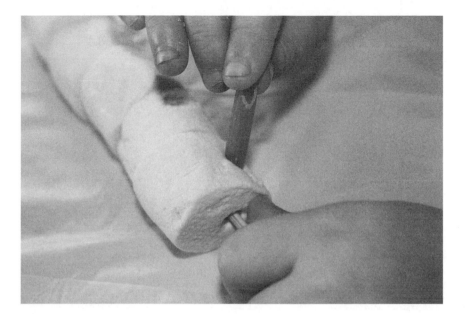

Step 3: Break a skewer into two pieces. Slide the skewer through the pasta to clean out any marshmallow pieces.

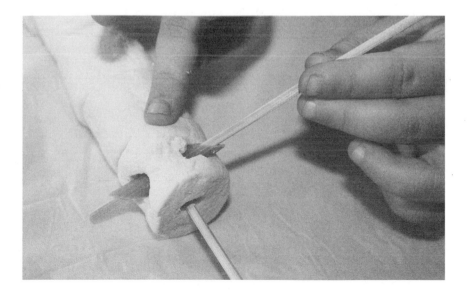

Step 4: Push one of the half pieces of skewer into a marshmallow. Do not push it all the way through.

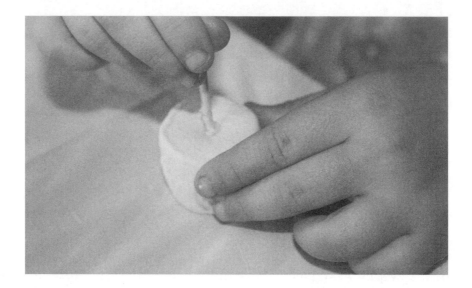

Step 5: Slide the bamboo axle through the penne pasta. Push a marshmallow onto the other side of the axle. Repeat for the other axle and wheels.

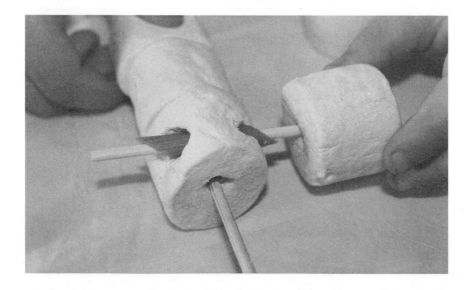

Step 6: Grab the back of the skewer to help steer your Mallow Magic racecar.

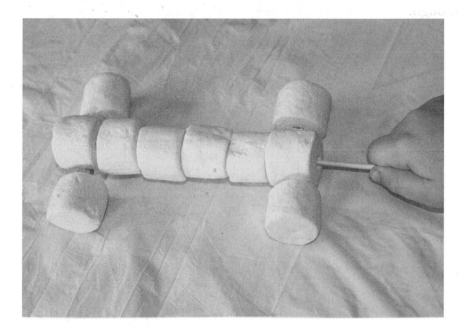

Additional Racecar Topics

Mallow Magic rolls very well but is not incredibly fast. Mallow Magic doesn't have very much weight, so it doesn't have very much potential energy when placed on a ramp. Mallow Magic also gets sticky in the summer since the marshmallows melt easily. But the long tail skewer makes it perfect when someone lights a fire. Toasted Mallow Magic would be a tasty treat.

SPUD RACER

A single potato is capable of rolling right off your dining room table.

Rolling Gear

Bamboo skewer
Raw potato
Wagon wheel pasta
Minimarshmallows or raisins
Mr. Potato Head parts or colored markers (optional)

Step 1: Break a bamboo skewer in half. This can be done by hand or, with an adult's help, you can cut it with a saw or knife.

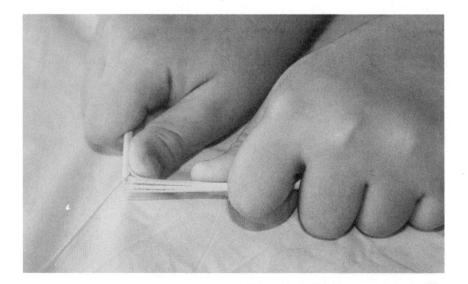

Step 2: Push the sharp end of the skewer through the front bottom of the potato. The skewer point is sharp, so be careful. Pull the sharp skewer out and replace with the other

half of the original skewer. Push the sharp point of the skewer through the back bottom of the potato. Make sure your axles are parallel to each other and parallel to the ground.

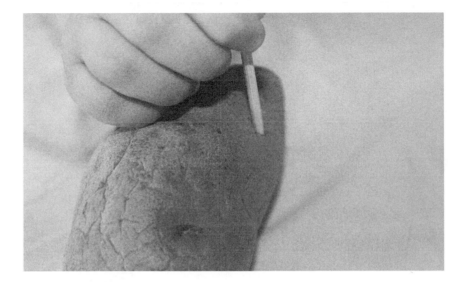

Step 3: Push a minimarshmallow or raisin onto the axle. Push it close to the body. This piece will help the wheel stay upright.

Step 4: Slide on a wagon wheel pasta followed by another minimarshmallow or raisin. Make sure the wagon wheel can roll freely.

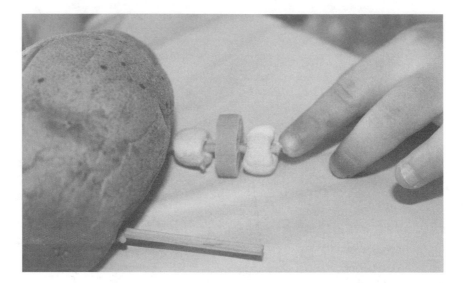

Step 5: Repeat Step 4 for all three remaining wheels.

Step 6: Have fun and decorate your spud racer. Mr. Potato Head pieces can be used, or you can just use colored markers. Add numbers and racing car stripes.

Additional Racecar Topics

The Spud Racer has a lot of potential energy on a ramp, so it will have a lot of kinetic energy at the bottom. And kinetic energy means speed. But the car doesn't have much ground clearance since wagon wheel pasta is small. The transition from the ramp to the ground might be hard. You can experiment and move the axles forward or backward to help with this if it is a problem. You can also try bigger wheels, like cookies, but you would lose points for this in a nutritional car contest.

GREEN MACHINE

A gravity-powered cucumber that will roll out in style.

Adult supervision required

Rolling Gear

Cucumber
Knife
Toothpicks
Raisins

Step 1: Slice four ½-inch thick slices off a cucumber. The slices will be your wheels, so you want them all about the same size.

Step 2: Poke a toothpick through the center of each cucumber wheel.

Step 3: Push the other end of the toothpick into the cucumber body.

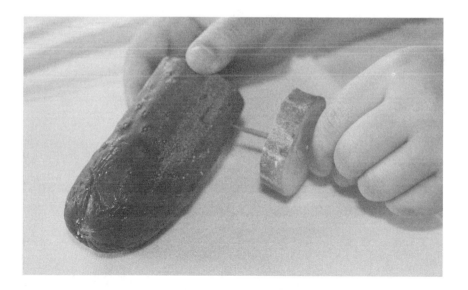

Step 4: Push a raisin onto the toothpick to act as a hub. Make sure the wheel can roll freely. You can also use Craisins or minimarshmallows as hubs.

Step 5: Repeat Steps 2 through 4 for the other three wheels.

Additional Racecar Topics

The Green Machine rolls well and has enough weight to get good speed at the bottom of a ramp. As with all edible cars, damage can occur as it hits the bottom of the ramp. Be careful to limit the number of test runs you do if you want to win. You can always make several Green Machines. The Green Machine would also score very high if the contest awarded points for nutritional value.

CHOCOLATE THUNDER

A candy-powered racecar is both fun and fattening.

Rolling Gear

Deli toothpicks
4 small Reese's cups or York Peppermint Patties
Raisins or marshmallows (optional)
Candy bar

Step 1: Poke a deli toothpick through the center of your candy wheel. Deli toothpicks have a decorative plastic end. You can also use regular toothpicks with raisins or mini-marshmallows on the end.

Step 2: Push the other end of the toothpick into the candy bar. Leave the candy bar wrapped so you can eat it later to celebrate your victory.

Step 3: Repeat for the other three wheels.

Additional Racecar Topics

This car rolls well, but the candy wheels will quickly start wobbling. The toothpick will make the axle hole bigger as it rolls, so limit your test runs with this edible racer.

BUN FUN

Use a hot dog bun to create a racer capable of rolling 10 feet or more.

Rolling Gear

Thick pretzel rod
Hot dog bun or sub roll
Striped shortbread cookies
Gummi Life Savers

Step 1: Break the pretzel rod in half.

Step 2: Use the broken end of the pretzel rod like a drill bit to drill through one end of the bun about 1 inch from the end.

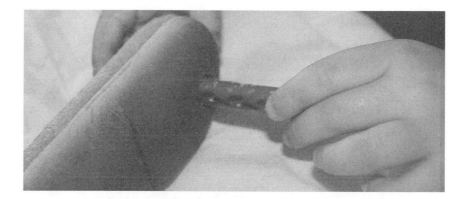

Step 3: Repeat with the other pretzel half at the other end of the bun.

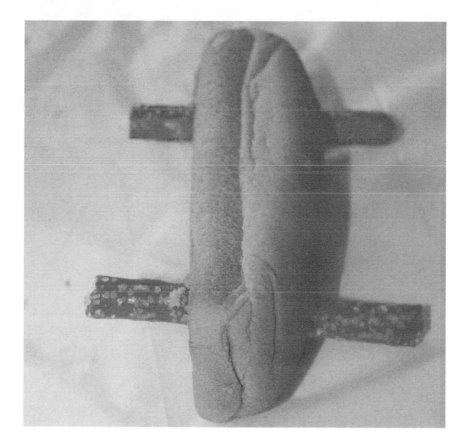

Step 4: Slide a striped shortbread cookie onto one of the axles.

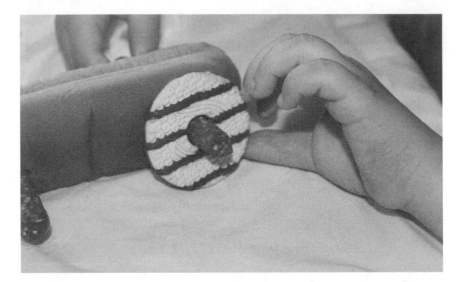

Step 5: Slide a Gummy Life Saver onto the pretzel rod to trap the cookie wheel.

Step 6: Repeat for all three remaining wheels. Make sure that the cookie wheels are free to roll.

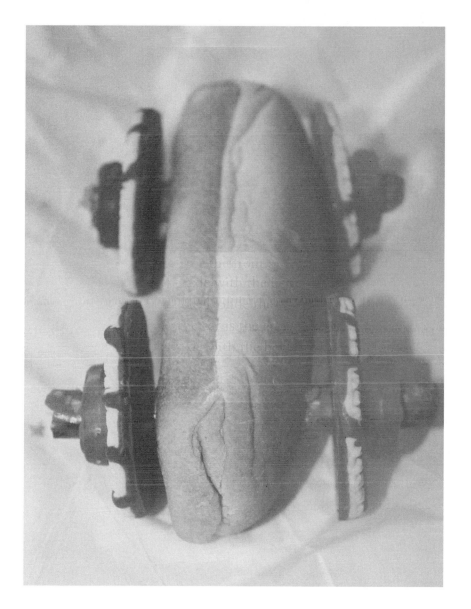

Additional Racecar Topics

You can try any cookies that have an open center, like chocolate marshmallow cookies. In the Bun Fun car shown here, the axles are toothpicks and the hubs are jelly beans. Whole wheat buns help the nutritional score, but the cookies and candy hurt the nutritional factor.

RICE CAR

The Rice Car will get you to the finish line first.

Rolling Gear

6 bamboo skewers
Marshmallow rice treats
Large round rice cakes
4 raisins

Step 1: Slide two bamboo skewers into the narrow end of a marshmallow rice treat. Insert the skewers into the middle and be careful to keep them parallel.

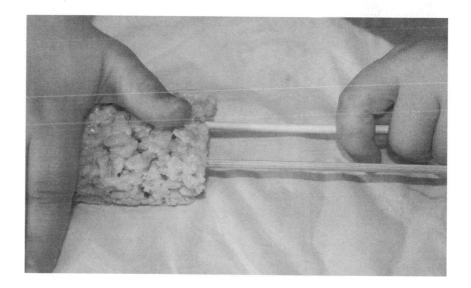

Step 2: Slide another marshmallow rice treat onto the skewers.

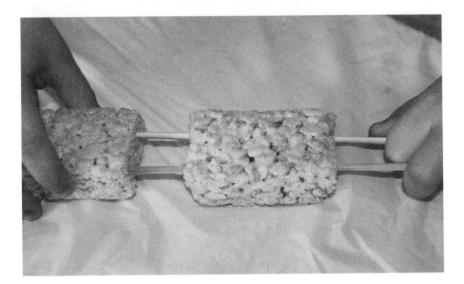

Step 3: Slide a third marshmallow rice treat onto the skewers. (Two treats may be enough if they are larger ones.)

Step 4: Use the heat of your hands to mold the treats together.

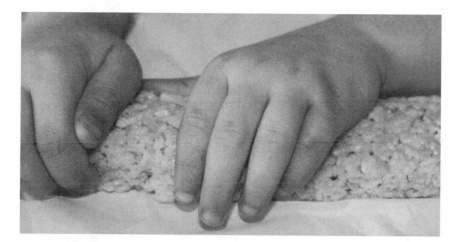

Step 5: If you use the large treats, you can simply push two axle skewers through the treats perpendicular to the body and skip to Step 7. If you use the small treats (as pictured), you will need to lay the axle skewers across the lower body and press them into the treats.

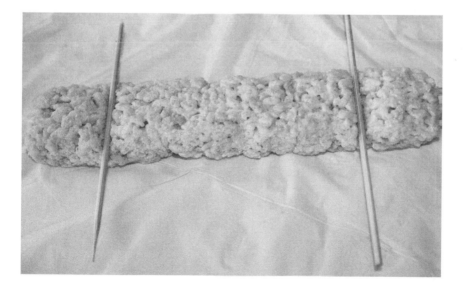

Step 6: Repeat Steps 1 through 3 to create the top of your Rice Car. Use the heat of your hands to mold the top onto the bottom.

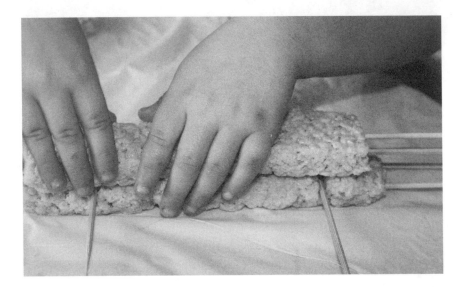

Step 7: Push a skewer through the center of each of the four large rice cakes.

Step 8: Twist the skewer to widen the center hole. You want the rice cake wheels to spin freely around the axle.

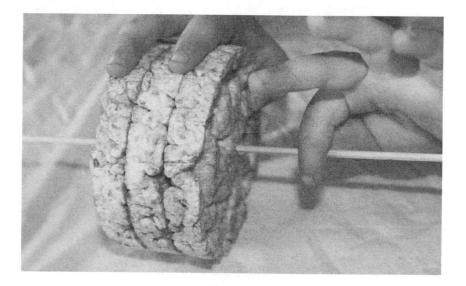

Step 9: Slide one wheel onto each side of both axles.

Step 10: Slide a raisin onto each side of both axles to act as hubs for the rice cake wheels.

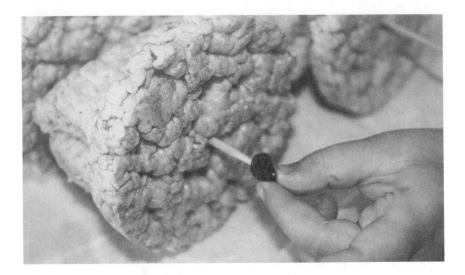

Step 11: Practice rolling the Rice Car. There are probably a limited number of times the Rice Car can survive an actual ramp, but holding the skewer will allow you to test it on a smooth surface.

Additional Racecar Topics

The Rice Car rolls well because of its large wheels. This is not the car for a hot summer day though, since the treats will melt quickly. You can also leave the treats in wrappers for the body of the car if you want to eat them later. If you leave the wrappers on, you will only make a single-deck car. The wrappers will help hold the skewers in place. If your car must be completely edible, thin pretzel sticks can act as axles. But skewers are stronger and more reliable, if allowed.

6
Gravity Racers

Racecars can be powered by the amazing force of gravity. Gravity is the force that pulls us all down. An object at the top of a hill has gravitational potential energy. The object has energy simply because of where it is—up high—and the fact that the object has weight. More weight and/or more height equals more energy. All you need is a ramp to launch these fun racecars.

BIRTHDAY CAR

Turn an old birthday card into a gravity-powered machine.

Adult supervision required

Rolling Gear

Old birthday (or other holiday) card

Scissors

Ruler

Pencil

Tape

4 plastic bottle tops

Drill and bits

Hot glue (optional)

Scrap of cardboard

4 nails

Step 1: Cut the front off an old birthday card. Fold the short end of the card over a ruler.

Step 2: Continue wrapping the card around the ruler. Pull it as tight as possible as you wrap it.

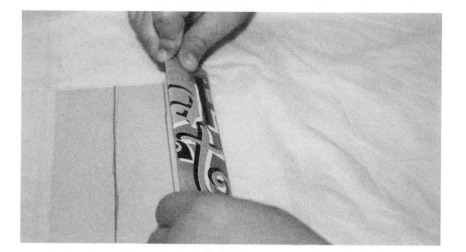

Step 3: Unroll the card and shape it into a long, rectangular tube. The front and back should be pretty square. It doesn't matter if some of the card overlaps. It actually makes the car body stronger, so don't trim off any excess. The overlap will be the bottom of the car.

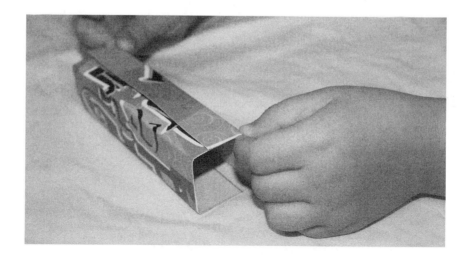

Step 4: Mark an X on the top of the car, which is the side opposite of the overlap. Open the body back up. Cut down the center of the tube to the section marked with the X. The following steps will create a cockpit and windshield.

Step 5: Cut 1 inch perpendicular to the previous cut, along the fold, toward the rear of the car. Repeat at the adjacent fold farther along the first cut. You are cutting two parallel slits the same length.

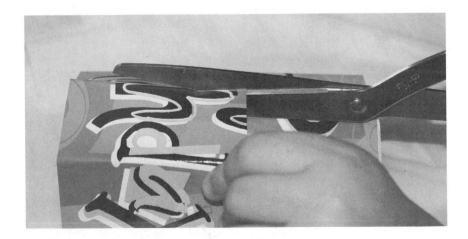

Step 6: Fold the piece down between the two cuts you just made. This will be the back of the cockpit.

Step 7: Now cut two parallel slits on the same folds, now cutting toward the front of the car. These slits should be about ½-inch long and will form the windshield.

Step 8: Fold the windshield up at about a 45 degree angle.

Step 9: Form the car back into the long rectangular tube. Use a small piece of tape to hold it together.

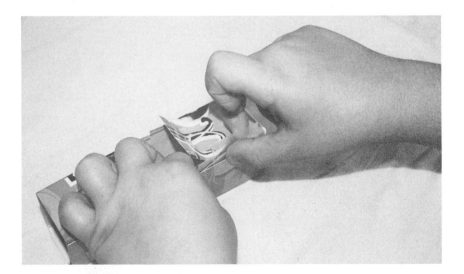

Step 10: Wrap long pieces of tape around the front and back of the Birthday Car.

Step 11: Use tape to repair the long cut created during the making of the cockpit.

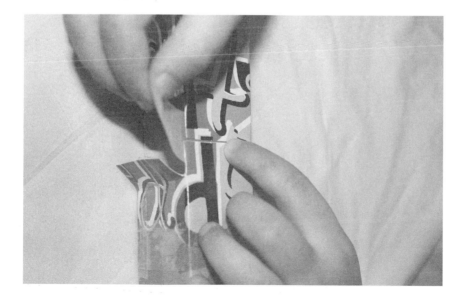

Step 12: Have an adult drill through the center of each of the four bottle caps. As an alternative, you can use hot glue to attach a nail head to the inside of each bottle cap.

Step 13: Lay your car on a scrap piece of cardboard and trace around the car bottom. Repeat this for a total of two cardboard pieces.

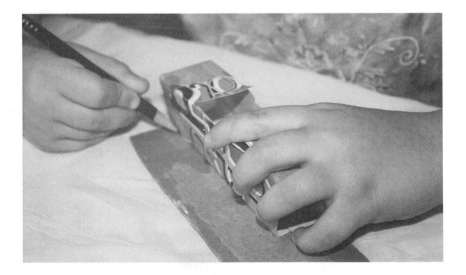

Step 14: Use scissors to cut out the cardboard. Cut on the inside of your tracing line. You want the cardboard pieces to be slightly smaller than the bottom of the Birthday Car.

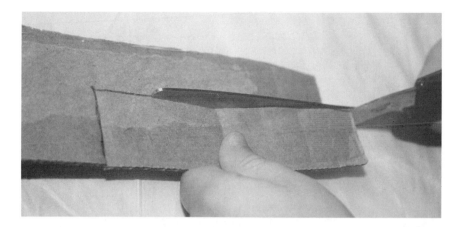

Step 15: Put one piece of cardboard inside the bottom of the Birthday Car. Place the other piece on the outside of the bottom. Push one end of a piece of tape inside the body onto the cardboard piece. Wrap the tape around onto the bottom piece of cardboard.

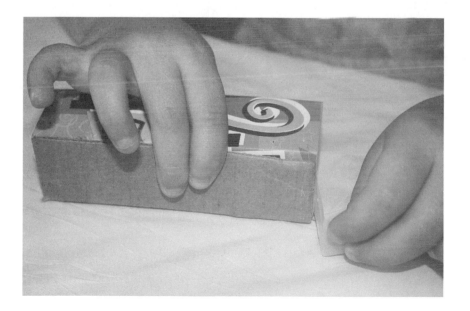

Step 16: Put a nail through the hole in the center of the bottle cap wheels. Slide the nail into the cardboard underneath the body. Repeat for all four wheels. If the nails are too long, the axles have to be staggered slightly.

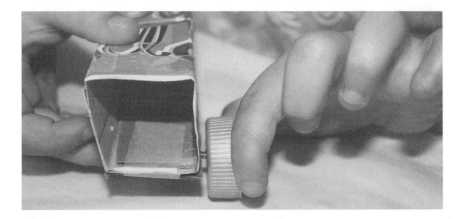

Step 17: Take your Birthday Car for a test ride. Put a toy in the cockpit to take a spin.

Additional Racecar Topics

Try a heavier toy to see if you get more speed at the bottom of a ramp. You can also try different size bottle caps for the wheels.

TRI-CAN RACER

Adult supervision required

Rolling Gear

2 rulers with notebook holes
3 small Pringles cans
Pencil
Drill and bits
3 nuts and bolts, 5 inches by ¼ inch
Washers

Step 1: Use a ruler to locate and mark the center of each Pringles can bottom and top.

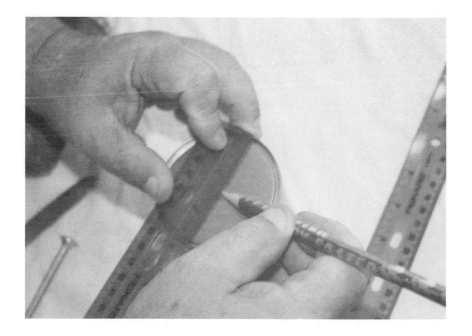

Step 2: With an adult's help, use a ⁵⁄₁₆ bit to drill a hole in the bottom of each can.

Step 3: Repeat for the plastic top of each can. It is easier to drill if the top is on the can.

Step 4: Drill the holes out on one of the rulers with the ⁵⁄₁₆ drill bit.

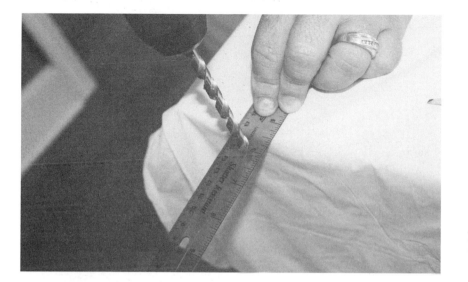

Step 5: Thread a bolt through each of the three holes in the other ruler. The bolts should fit, but you will have to thread them through the hole. If the bolts don't fit, get an adult to help drill the holes larger in this ruler.

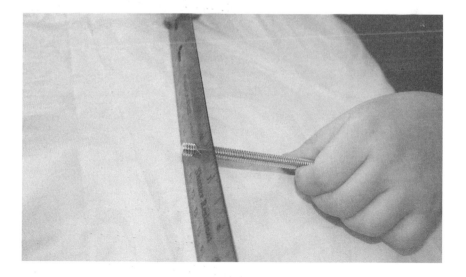

Step 6: Slide a washer onto each bolt. Now slide a Pringles can onto each bolt. Reverse the direction of the center Pringles can so the car will roll straighter.

Step 7: Slide a washer onto each bolt on top of the Pringles cans.

Step 8: Slide the drilled ruler onto the three bolts.

Step 9: Thread a nut onto each bolt and tighten. Leave the bolts loose enough so the Pringles cans roll.

Step 10: Now you are ready to roll. Find an incline and let the racer go.

Additional Racecar Topics

Set a target up on the floor and see if you can hit it.

TRI-CAN HAULER

Rolling Gear

Tri-Can Racer (page 165)   Scissors

Ruler   Pen

Old cereal box   Tape

Step 1: You are going to create a box for the center of the Tri-Can Racer, which you built earlier. Remove the center can from the Tri-Can Racer. Measure the length and width of the rectangle formed by the two rulers and the two cans. Open up an old cereal box by cutting along one edge to lay it flat. Draw a rectangle with a width that equals the measurement between the rulers. The length measurement should be ½ inch less than the distance between the two cans.

Step 2: Draw a rectangle along each long side of the big rectangle with the same length as the big rectangle and a width of 1 inch. Draw an identical 1-inch-wide rectangle along the side of these rectangles. Along each short side of the big rectangle draw rectangles with the same length as the short side of the big rectangle and a width of 1 inch.

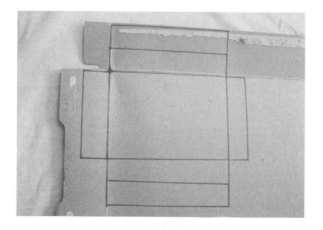

Step 3: Use the scissors to cut along the outside line of all the lines just created. When you are finished cutting, the middle part should look like this.

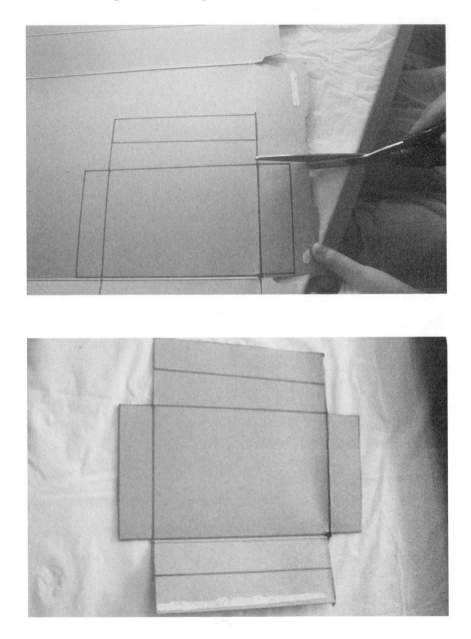

Step 4: Fold along each line of the big rectangle.

Step 5: Fold down both long, skinny side rectangles so they stick out from the box.

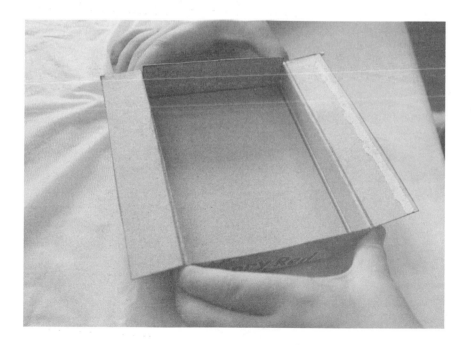

Step 6: Use tape to secure each bottom corner of the box.

Step 7: Place the box between the two rulers. Bend each long side rectangle over the ruler and secure to the ruler.

Step 8: Now the Tri-Can Hauler is ready to go. Put your favorite action figure in and you are off to the races.

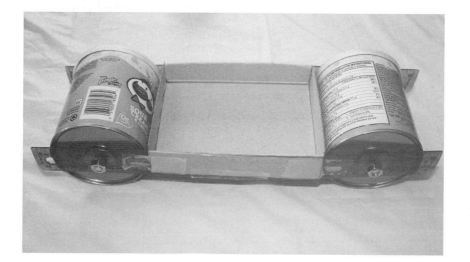

Additional Racecar Topics

The Tri-Can Hauler is all about carrying the load. Try to see how much weight you can safely carry. See if the weight in the box affects the hauler's speed at the bottom of a ramp.

MAC-N-CHEESE ROLLER

Turn an empty box into a recycled rolling machine.

Rolling Gear

Corrugated cardboard

Pen

CD or jar lid

Scissors

Empty mac-n-cheese box

Hole punch

Tape

2 straws

Step 1: Trace four wheels on a piece of cardboard. You can use a CD or a jar lid.

Step 2: Mark the center of each wheel. Now cut the wheels out. Cutting cardboard is difficult. To make this easier, cut a square containing each wheel and then trim the wheels to the correct size. This is easier than holding the entire cardboard piece.

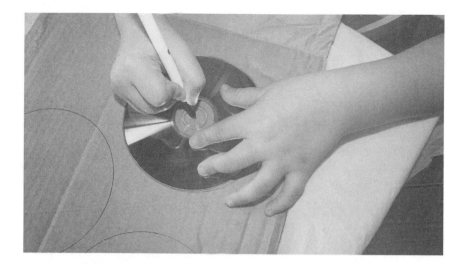

Step 3: Open the top and bottom of an empty mac-n-cheese box. Make a pen mark ½ inch from the back of the box on the top and bottom of both skinny sides of the box. Use a hole punch to make a hole near each mark. Slide the hole punch all the way until it is stopped by the box. This will ensure the axles are perfectly parallel. Use the ½-inch mark as a guide to keep the axles level to the ground.

Step 4: Refold the box into its original shape and secure each corner with tape.

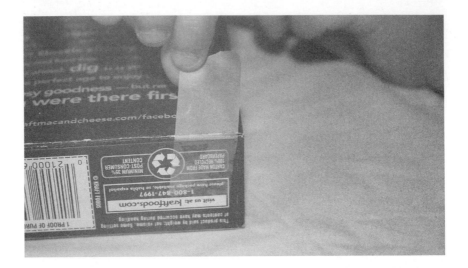

Step 5: Use the point of a pair of scissors to create a hole in each wheel. Make the hole the same size as the straw. The wheel can be super tight or a little loose for this roller. If the hole is too big though, the racecar won't stand up straight. Be careful with the scissors.

Step 6: Slide the straw through the mac-n-cheese box. Slide one wheel onto the straw and wrap tape around the end of the straw axle to hold it in place.

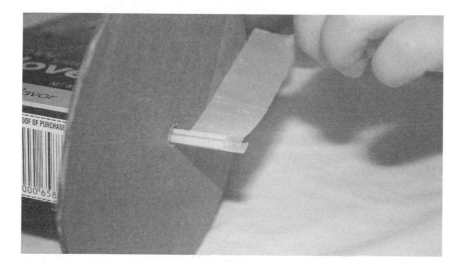

Step 7: Slide the other wheel on and repeat. Make sure the wheels are upright and leave only a little space from the sides of the box. The wheels should spin freely.

Step 8: Repeat for the other axle and you are ready to roll.

Additional Racecar Topics

Try changing the angle of the ramp. Also try adding weight to the top of the box. A great way to do this is to tape coins onto the box. Build two cars with different size wheels and have a race.

7
Racecar Launchers

Build fun launchers to give your racers a fantastic start.

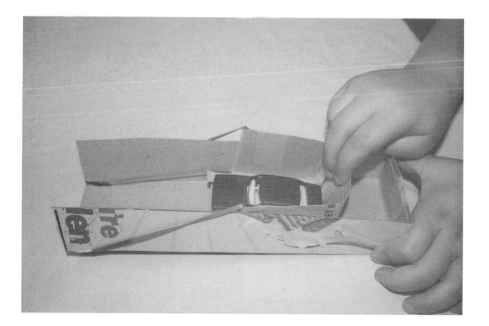

HOTTER THAN HOT WHEELS LAUNCHER

This rubber band–powered launcher will shoot your toy cars across the room.

Rolling Gear

Empty cereal box

Pen

Ruler

Scissors

Tape

2 rubber bands

Step 1: Draw a line 1½ inches from the corner of the skinny side of a cereal box. Repeat on the other side of the box. Cut along the line on both sides.

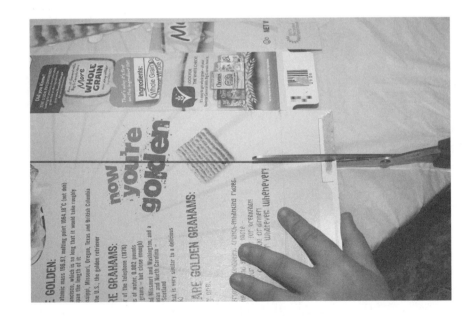

Step 2: On the piece of box you just cut off, draw a line 3 inches up from one end. Cut directly across the line.

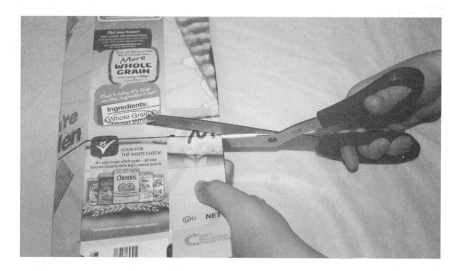

Step 3: Along the flat cut edge of the cardboard, measure in from the side 1½ inches. Make a cut ½-inch long at each mark. You will use these flaps later.

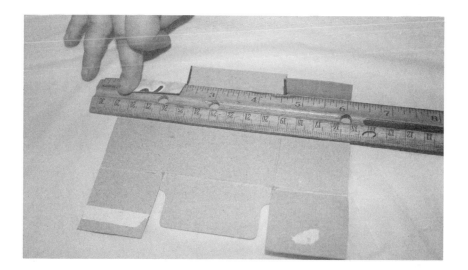

Step 4: You are now going to narrow the sled. Mark a line ¼ inch from one of the original corners of the cereal box. Cut along that line.

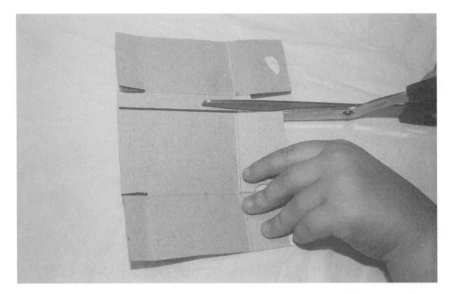

Step 5: Overlap these two pieces by ¼ inch. Place a piece of tape along this entire overlap.

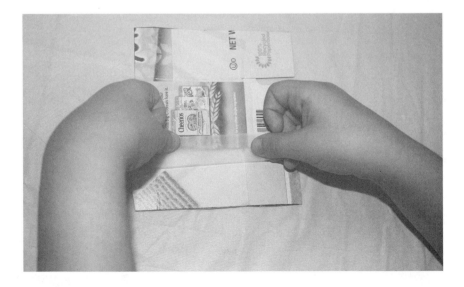

Step 6: Turn this piece over and tape the other side.

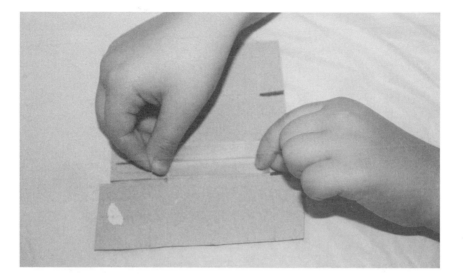

Step 7: Now fold the cereal box corner back together. Fold up one side and hold it in place.

Step 8: Fold the other side up and tape the corner back together. You are left with an original cereal box corner that is narrower than the original.

Step 9: Fold out one of the small flaps you created in Step 3 and place a rubber band around it.

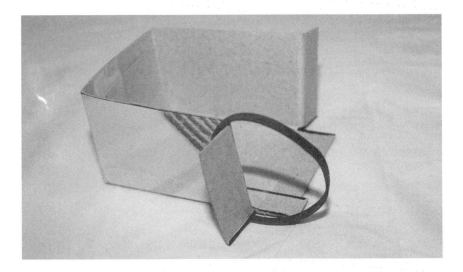

Step 10: Fold the small flap toward the rear of the sled and pull the rubber band tight.

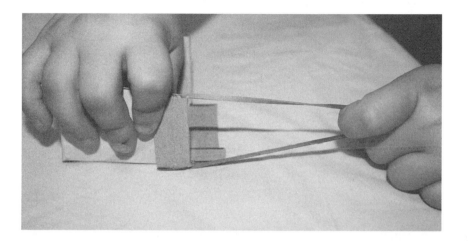

Step 11: Secure the small flap to the sled with a piece of tape. This will capture the rubber band. Repeat with another rubber band for the other side of the sled.

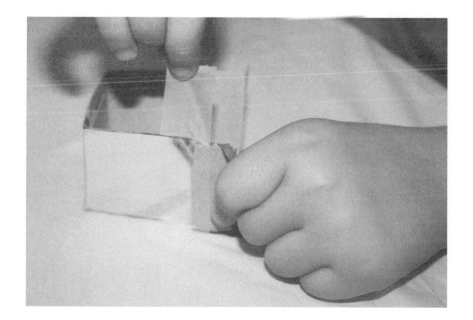

Step 12: Now build the launcher with the other piece of the long edge of the cereal box. Fold up the original corners and secure with tape.

Step 13: Cut a ½-inch slit up each corner of the open end of the launcher.

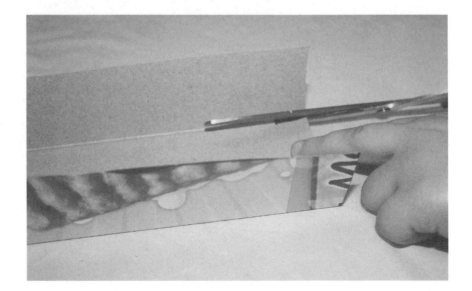

Step 14: Put the sled inside the launcher and pull the rubber bands into the slots you just cut.

Step 15: Pull the sled back so that the rubber bands slide all the way into the slots.

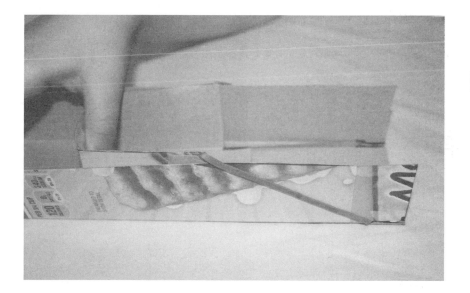

Step 16: Now it is time to launch some cars. Put a car in the sled. Use one hand to hold the launcher. Pull the sled back. When you let go of the sled, the car will zoom off.

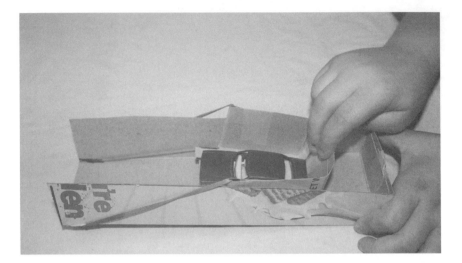

Additional Racecar Topics

Elastic energy from the rubber bands is what makes cars race across the floor. Try different rubber bands. They can easily be changed by removing the tape on the sled and then replacing them. Try different cars to find your hottest Hot Wheel.

CEREAL RAMP

Turn a cereal box into a fun, single-car race ramp.

Rolling Gear

Empty cereal box

Pen

Scissors

Yardstick

Tape

Step 1: Draw a giant U on the front and back of an empty cereal box. Keep the U about 1 inch from the corners of the box. Cut out the U on each side with the scissors.

Step 2: Use the scissors to make a diagonal cut from the U to the corners of the box. The cut should go as far into the corners as possible.

Step 3: With the cuts made, you can now unfold the Cereal Ramp. The corners might tear a little as you straighten the box if you couldn't cut all the way to the corner. That is OK.

Step 4: To give the Cereal Ramp some support, use a yardstick (or meter stick). Put the ramp all the way at one end. Wrap a piece of tape all the way over the end to secure it.

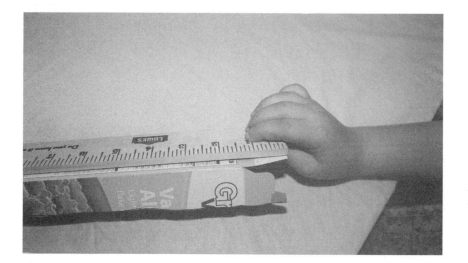

Step 5: Secure the other end to the top of the yardstick with tape.

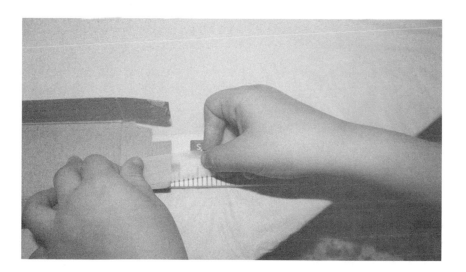

Step 6: Now you are ready to launch cars. Place a car at the top of the Cereal Ramp and let it go.

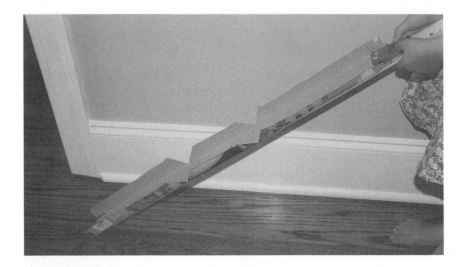

Additional Racecar Topics

The starting height is the key to great speed for the Cereal Ramp. More height equals more gravitational potential energy (GPE). And more GPE means more speed at the bottom. Try different angles, which will give you different starting heights. Be careful though—maximum starting height will result in a big crash as the car hits the floor.

JUICE BOX LAUNCHER

Power your cars with three empty juice boxes that shoot the cars across the room.

Rolling Gear

3 empty juice boxes	Scissors
Corrugated cardboard	Duct tape
Marker	2 rubber bands

Step 1: Rinse out three empty juice boxes. Lay the three juice boxes on a piece of corrugated cardboard with their long edges together. Trace around the outside edges with a marker. The boxes do not have to be super tight together as you trace.

Step 2: Use the scissors to cut out two pieces of cardboard the same size as your tracing. Cut on the outside of the line so the center box will be free to move later.

Step 3: Sandwich two juice boxes between the two pieces of cardboard. Slide the juice boxes out slightly so that the third juice box will be loose in the middle. You can test it before you tape it in the next step.

Step 4: Wrap duct tape around the front and back of your juice box sandwich. It is easiest to use two strips for the front and two for the back.

Step 5: Take a strip of duct tape and create a thin strip by folding it. Fold ⅓ in on the sticky side. Fold the other ⅓ on top of that piece. This is your pull strap for your launcher. Put two equal size rubber bands onto the handle and test fit it to the center box.

Step 6: Wrap duct tape around the center box and trap the handle to both sides.

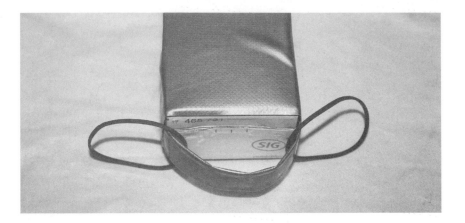

Step 7: Take a thin strip of duct tape off the roll. Duct tape can be torn for the correct length and will also tear down the middle to create thinner strips. You can also use scissors. Stick one of the rubber bands on the launcher handle 1 inch from the end of the duct tape. Fold over that end of the tape, capturing the rubber band. There should be some sticky part left.

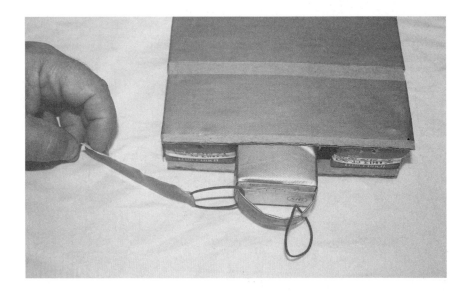

Step 8: Pull the sticky part and attach it to the side of the juice box sandwich.

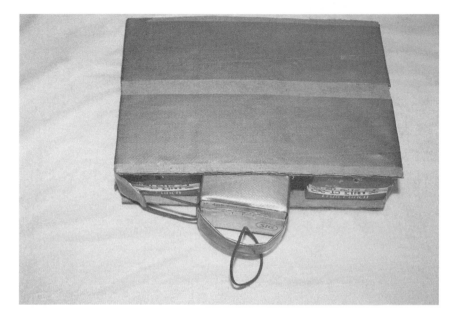

Step 9: Repeat Steps 7 and 8 for the other side of the handle.

Step 10: You are now ready to load the launcher. Slide the car in from the front side while you pull the handle back.

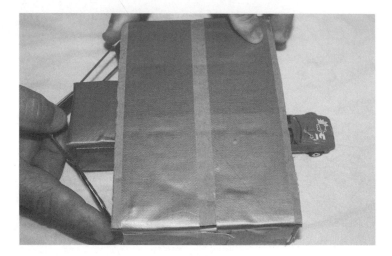

Step 11: Use one hand to hold the Juice Box Launcher steady. Pull back with the other hand and launch your car.

Additional Racecar Topics

Try adding more rubber bands to each side. Try different cars to see which cars roll the best.

MEGA RAMP

Give all your cars a great start to have fun races.

Rolling Gear

Large cardboard box lid   Ruler
Scissors   Doorstop (optional)

Note: A large cardboard lid works best for this project. These large lids can be found on almost all ready-to-assemble furniture boxes. You can also make your own by taping two or three smaller boxes together. Even a large, flat sheet of cardboard can be used. Be creative and see the fun in all the shapes of cardboard around you. To see an epically large ramp go to YouTube (with permission) and search "Hot Wheels Track! Hot Wheel Cars."

Step 1: Take one end of the cardboard lid and cut the corners so that end will lie flat.

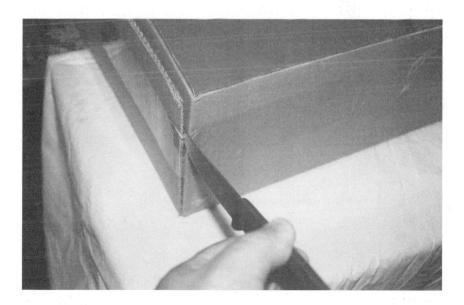

Step 2: Place the other end of the cardboard on a chair.

Step 3: Use a ruler to give your cars an even start for a race. Hold the ruler in front of the cars. Pull it up quickly and let the cars go. You can also just let cars go with your hand.

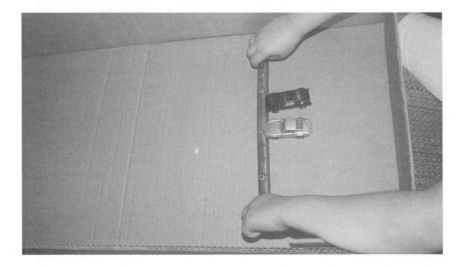

Optional Step 4: To launch your cars in the air, slide a doorstop under the bottom flap.

Additional Racecar Topics

Have fun with your ramp designs. Tape several boxes together to create ramps that can curve. Challenge your friends to racing championships.

PULL-BACK RACER

Use a rubber band to launch your cars across the floor.

Rolling Gear

Paper clip

Toy car

Tape

Rubber band

Cardboard scrap

Step 1: Unfold the small loop of a paper clip. Twist the small loop so it is perpendicular to the rest of the clip.

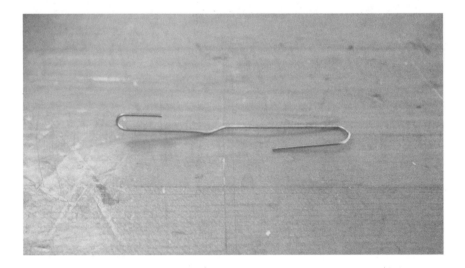

Step 2: Lay your toy car upside down. Use a piece of tape (or a rubber band) to secure the clip to the bottom of the car. The bent hook from Step 1 should face the front .

of the car, and the opening of the hook should face the floor when the car is right-side up.

Step 3: Hook a rubber band inside the paper clip hook to make sure the clip is in the correct position. Reposition if necessary.

Step 4: Put a small piece of cardboard on your surface. Tape it down. Use a piece of tape to secure the other end of the rubber band. Pull back your racecar and let it go.

Additional Racecar Topics

The rubber band and your muscles supply the power for this launcher. Try different size rubber bands. Try different cars. Testing different brand rubber bands would be a great science fair project. Most of all, have fun.